To Charles
who really did
help with this.
Peter Vannan

SOVIET STRATEGY IN
SOUTHERN AFRICA

SOVIET STRATEGY IN SOUTHERN AFRICA

Gorbachev's Pragmatic Approach

PETER VANNEMAN

HOOVER INSTITUTION PRESS

Stanford University
Stanford, California

The Hoover Institution on War, Revolution and Peace, founded at
Stanford University in 1919 by President Herbert Hoover,
is an interdisciplinary research center for advanced study on
domestic and international affairs in the twentieth century.
The views expressed in its publications are entirely those of the
authors and do not necessarily reflect the views of the staff,
officers, or Board of Overseers of the Hoover Institution.

Hoover Press Publication 390
Copyright 1990 by the Board of Trustees of the
Leland Stanford Junior University

All rights reserved. No part of this publication may be reproduced,
stored in a retrieval system, or transmitted in any form
or by any means, electronic, mechanical, photocopying, recording,
or otherwise, without written permission of the publisher.

First printing, 1990
96 95 94 93 92 91 90   9 8 7 6 5 4 3 2 1
Simultaneous first paperback printing, 1990
96 95 94 93 92 91 90   9 8 7 6 5 4 3 2 1
Manufactured in the United States of America
Printed on acid-free paper

Library of Congress Cataloging-in-Publication Data
Vanneman, Peter.
Soviet strategy in Southern Africa : Gorbachev's pragmatic
approach / Peter Vanneman.
p.   cm.
Includes bibliographical references.
ISBN 0-8179-8901-3 (alk. paper).
ISBN 0-8179-8902-1 (pbk. : alk. paper)
1. Africa, Southern—Foreign relations—Soviet Union.   2. Soviet
Union—Foreign relations—Africa, Southern.   3. Soviet Union—
Foreign relations—1985-   I. Title.
DT1105.S65V36   1990   89-28456
327.47068—dc20   CIP

CONTENTS

Acknowledgments vii

Introduction ix

1. THE POLICY PROCESS: Decisionmaking and Implementation 1

2. SOUTH AFRICA: Armed Struggle, Diplomacy, Duplicity 13

3. THE AFRICAN NATIONAL CONGRESS: A Complex and Evolving Soviet Relationship 25

4. NAMIBIA: The USSR and SWAPO 37

5. ANGOLA: Three Decades of Involvement 45

6. MOZAMBIQUE: The USSR as Rearguard 58

7. THE NONALIGNED STATES: Constraints and Opportunities 70

8. COERCIVE DIPLOMACY: Tactics and Instruments 81

9. SOVIET STRATEGY: Motivations, Perceptions, Continuity 96

Notes 109

Selected Bibliography 133

Index 137

ACKNOWLEDGMENTS

Many institutions and individuals encouraged this endeavor, but, of course, none bear any responsibility for the final product. Above all the support provided by the Hoover Institution on War, Revolution and Peace at Stanford University and the Fulbright Institute of International Relations at the University of Arkansas enabled this project to come to fruition. The Kennan Institute for Advanced Russian Studies also provided a fellowship for the initial study of opinion groups in the Soviet-African policy process. My stint in Tanzania as a management analyst on President Julius Nyerere's staff, which kindled an early interest in Africa, was supported by the Ford Foundation.

I would like to thank especially Ambassador Richard Staar, coordinator of the International Studies Program at Hoover, and Dr. L. H. Gann, and Dr. Peter Duignan, distinguished Africanists and senior fellows at that institution, as well as Thomas Henriksen, deputy director; the guidance of the superb staff of the Hoover Press proved indispensable, especially Ann Wood, senior editor; Lenore McCracken, marketing manager; and Andrew Ould, copy editor. As a visiting scholar, I was able to enjoy and use Hoover's vast library and intellectual resources under the Discretionary Grant Program, Department of State, Soviet–Eastern European Research and Training Act of 1983, Title VIII. At the Fulbright Institute, the support and encouragement of the director, Hoyt Purvis, was invaluable. Betty Skinner, its administrative assistant, unflaggingly bore the burden of producing the first draft, which Kathryn Cantrell edited.

The works and counsel of Vernon Aspaturian, director of the Soviet and Slavic Language and Area Center of Pennsylvania State University, Jerry Hough, professor of political science at Duke University, and Dr. Seth Tillman, research professor of diplomacy at Georgetown, informed and inspired me over the years. The helpful friends in Africa and the USSR are too numerous to list here. Steven White provided a forum for the initial version of chapters 2 and 3 in the September 1989 volume of his excellent journal, *Coexistence*.

My greatest debt of gratitude is to my wife, Susan, whose advice and encouragement at every stage made this work possible.

INTRODUCTION

The more assertive foreign policy of the Reagan administration gradually arrested the momentum of Soviet strategy in southern Africa as the 1980s drew to a close. By tying Soviet behavior in the Third World to issues of greater importance to Moscow and by aiding the Angolan insurgents, the United States raised the costs and risks of the Kremlin's predominantly military strategy, thus stimulating a Soviet reassessment that stressed less costly political and diplomatic stratagems.

Nevertheless, despite the successful U.S. initiatives, the USSR's long-range optimism in the Third World is probably greatest in southern Africa for multifarious reasons, but foremost are the opportunities presented by the area's chronic instability. Soviet influence in the Third World is greatest where the regimes are most insecure, and insecurity is the hallmark of many regimes in southern Africa.

Since 1983 the staffs of the Soviet embassies in Mozambique, Zimbabwe, and Botswana have tripled, and there is a new and relatively large embassy in tiny landlocked Lesotho, inside South Africa itself. In addition, the Moscow missions of both the South African and the Namibian insurgents were upgraded and expanded in 1987–1989. There are special sections in the International Department of the Communist Party of the Soviet Union (CPSU) and the Foreign Ministry for southern Africa. The largest section of the propaganda department of the KGB has been the one for southern Africa.

In the mid-1980s the USSR poured about $1 billion worth of military equipment per year into Angola, and large numbers of Soviet advisers had been fighting with its troops down to the battalion level. In spring 1988, Cuba rapidly deployed a mechanized force of over 10,000 troops to Angola, bringing its troop total to 58,000 or more.

Across the continent in Mozambique, the Soviet-dominated Council for Mutual Economic Assistance (CMEA) signed the first agreements with any southern African country, and for the first time the USSR attended Southern African Development Coordinating Council (SADCC) meetings. In 1989 almost one thousand students returned to Mozambique after completing seven years of education in East Germany.

Relatively speaking, Marxist-Leninist ideology may be taken more seriously in southern Africa than in any other Third World region, although even there, as this study demonstrates, its relevance is increasingly suspect, especially in the economic arena. Nevertheless, in the eyes of some Soviet leaders southern Africa may represent an area where opportunities for pursuing the class struggle are still available. Although new thinking implies greater pragmatism, southern Africa provides unusual opportunities for the USSR to validate its residual credentials as a revolutionary state. There are few parts of the world where communist theories about the ultimate inevitability of revolution seem more applicable than the Republic of South Africa. But most Soviet Africanists do not expect a successful violent revolution in the foreseeable future. Nevertheless, Mikhail Gorbachev is the first CPSU general secretary to meet with the leader of the insurgent African National Congress (ANC) of South Africa.

Whether Soviet optimism about southern Africa is warranted depends above all on the region's stability. The conclusion of a U.S.-brokered agreement among Angola, South Africa, and Cuba (with the USSR as observer) in December 1988 may mitigate the chronic instability in Namibia and Angola, especially if the aggressive, persistent, and imaginative U.S. policies continue.

However, the Republic of South Africa is the major player in this area. Despite the success of South African security forces in controlling unrest, the ongoing crisis over the slow pace of reform of that nation's system of racial discrimination casts a shadow over the entire region and attracts disproportionate Soviet attention, given the relatively peripheral nature of the area in Moscow's global priorities.

There are some encouraging signs—such as the release of Nelson Mandela—that negotiations among all the major forces in South African society could ultimately lead to a more stable and just sociopolitical system. In the past the USSR clearly opposed and even feared that such a process of negotiation would undermine its influence, but Soviet behavior in 1987–1990 suggests that the Gorbachev regime has opted for diplomatic and political stratagems as the best means for promoting its interests in the short run, given the reordering of its priorities toward domestic reconstruction. What is likely, then, is the continuation of an opportunistic Soviet strategy to enhance Moscow's influence in the region and around the world that will focus more on public diplomacy and political stratagems and less on violence to minimize the risk of a U.S. reaction and an escalation of counterintervention.

This study of the massive Soviet/proxy involvement in the southern African region focuses particularly on Soviet strategy as reflected in Soviet behavior. The first chapter describes the policy process and especially the growth of the southern African apparatus both in Moscow and in the region. The next three chapters analyze Soviet strategy in South Africa and Namibia, stressing the central importance of Soviet backing for the insurgents, the ANC and the South-West Africa People's Organization (SWAPO). The following two chapters describe Soviet strategy toward its two Afro-Marxist clients: Angola and Mozambique. Chapter 6 recounts the quiet, but dramatic, expansion of Soviet involvement with the region's nonaligned states during the 1980s. The two concluding chapters examine Soviet diplomatic initiatives in the late 1980s and Soviet strategic interests in minerals and military facilities as well as the orchestrated deployment of the Soviet Union's elaborate congeries of proxies and auxiliaries.

Over the last two decades, Soviet behavior in southern Africa reflects a relatively consistent strategy: a series of carefully calibrated initiatives calculated to advance both the global and the regional interests of the USSR.

SOVIET STRATEGY IN SOUTHERN AFRICA

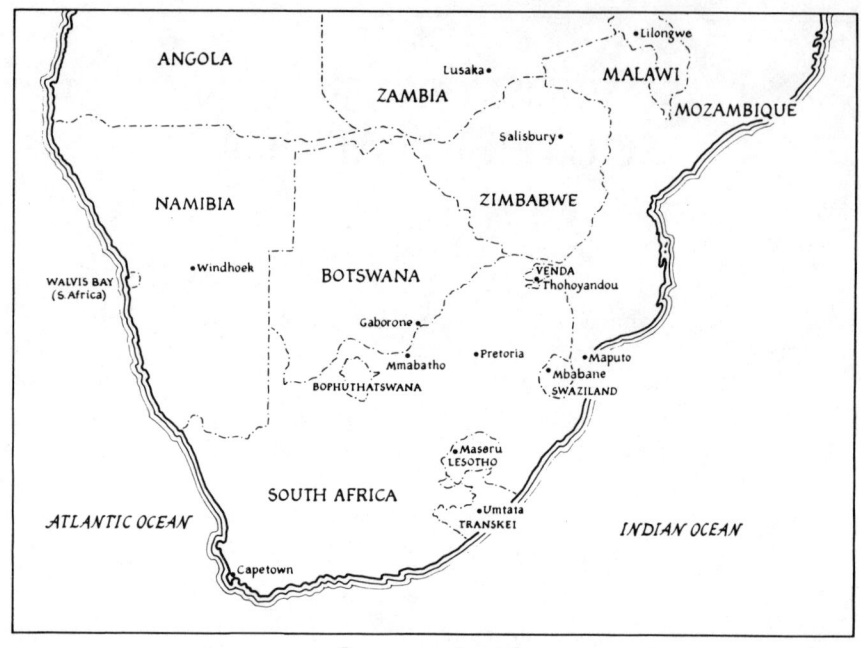

SOUTHERN AFRICA

1

THE POLICY PROCESS

Decision Making and Implementation

The growing importance of southern Africa in Soviet foreign policy was symbolized by the meeting between General Secretary Mikhail S. Gorbachev and the late president of Mozambique, Samora Machel, at the funeral of CPSU leader Konstantin Chernenko in March 1985. Gorbachev had just been elevated to head the CPSU. He did not meet with the president of Syria, an important Soviet client. That he found time to meet with the president of faraway Mozambique at this busy occasion is significant. The Soviet leader also took time to meet with President Machel at the 27th Party Congress a year later. When President Machel died in a plane crash in 1986, Gorbachev sent a 40-member Soviet delegation, including then Politburo member Geidar A. Aliyev, to the funeral. In addition, Gorbachev had appointed N. K. Dybenko as ambassador to Mozambique, the first CPSU Central Committee member to hold a diplomatic post in the region.

By the beginning of 1988, two members of the ruling Politburo had had significant experience with southern Africa, and there is evidence that the region is discussed at Politburo meetings.[1] As a further symbol of Moscow's concern for Africa, Gorbachev had appointed three deputy foreign ministers for Africa instead of one.

Although it was generally assumed that Gorbachev is relatively inexperienced in foreign policy, particularly in the Third World, he did serve as chairman of the Foreign Affairs Commission of the Supreme Soviet, an important post occupied by party leader Yuri V. Andropov before him and Mikhail A. Suslov, for years the leading party ideologist and theoretician. In this capacity Gorbachev persuaded the Supreme Soviet to adopt resolutions calling for more-sophisticated economic aid to "liberated" countries like Mozambique. This foreshadowed his new policy in the region, which is designed to derive as much advantage as possible from Soviet initiatives by stressing public diplomacy.[2]

The Decision Makers

Although southern Africa is not central to Soviet policy, the USSR is reasonably well informed about regional conditions. Soviet expertise on Africa has mushroomed since Nikita S. Khrushchev's time, and both the leadership and the Soviet officials in the party-state apparatus and the bureaucracy in the field have considerable experience with African affairs, which was not the case when Soviet initiatives in the Congo in the early 1960s culminated in a complete debacle. The contrast between the conquest of Angola in 1976 by fifteen thousand Cuban troops supplied and supported by the USSR and the Congo disaster reflects in part the increasing experience and sophistication of Soviet decision makers.

In 1977, Nikolai V. Podgorny, the then president of the USSR, toured Africa, and Andrei V. Kirilenko, a leading Politburo member, visited Angola in 1978.[3] Foreign Minister Eduard A. Shevardnadze (now a full Politburo member) met with Namibian insurgent leader Sam Nujoma in 1984, and Gorbachev met twice, in 1985 and 1986, on significant occasions with Mozambique's president. In June 1986, the 40-member Soviet delegation attended the funeral of Mozambique's president. There have been many other meetings of importance between Soviet and southern African leaders, but these were highly publicized occasions designed to signal Soviet commitment in a dramatic fashion.

By the late 1980s two members of the Politburo had some southern African experience: General Secretary Gorbachev, who had dealt with southern Africa in the Supreme Soviet and had met with southern African leaders, and Foreign Minister Shevardnadze, who has met regularly with southern African insurgents and leaders. That two important Politburo members have some acquaintance with southern African issues suggests a vigorous and pragmatic approach to the region.

The Southern African Policy Advisers

As early as 1971 more than three hundred Soviet scholars were studying Africa, and by the late 1980s numerous commentators and journalists had become known for their African expertise.[4] This represented a major step forward from the mid-1950s, when Ivan I. Potekhin, the dean of Soviet Africanists, became the first Soviet scholar allowed to pursue research in sub-Saharan Africa.[5] Even by 1988, however, no Soviet Africanist had set foot in that most important country, the Republic of South Africa. But Boris A. Asoyan, the ambassador to Lesotho, a small landlocked country entirely surrounded by the Republic of South Africa, had been inviting South African academics to lectures and discussions at his embassy, and South African academics and journalists have been traveling to the USSR, even though the two states have no diplomatic relations. In 1988 the South African government itself escorted a Soviet journalist around the republic.[6]

Four think tanks study Africa extensively: the Institute of the USA and Canada, the Oriental Institute, the Institute of the World Economy and International Relations (IMEMO), and the Africa Institute of the USSR Academy of Sciences. All except the last take a globalist view of African affairs, although individual scholars do differ within each institute. Politburo member Alexander N. Yakovlev, chief of the new Foreign Affairs Commission, headed IMEMO from 1983 to 1985 and was replaced by Yevgeny A. Primakov, generally recognized as a leading proponent of a globalist, geopolitical view of Africa and the Third World. Like Yakovlev, Primakov emphasized the strategic factors in an inevitable power struggle with the United States.[7]

The Southern African Apparatus of the International Department of the CPSU

The ruling Politburo has many sources of information to aid its decision making on southern Africa, but the most important is the International Department (I.D.) of the Party Secretariat, which coordinates and collates information from other organs, including the Foreign Ministry and the KGB. Of course, Foreign Minister Shevardnadze sits on the Politburo and is not dependent on the I.D. for information. Party Secretary Yakovlev, however, is Gorbachev's key foreign policy adviser, according to Vernon Aspaturian.[8]

One top deputy in the I.D. who is knowledgeable about southern Africa[9] is Karen A. Brutents, who has written widely about insurgencies in the Third World, although he is primarily an expert on the Middle East. He was promoted to first deputy under Gorbachev. A review of his writings suggests that he, like Yakovlev, advocates an offensive policy of anti-imperialism and aggravation of contradictions within the capitalist world, even as he emphasizes building ties with important capitalist states in the Third World. The demotion of another deputy, Rotislav Ulyanovsky, an authentic Africanist who has written about southern Africa for years, seems to reflect a more global policy orientation for African policy. Another deputy, Petr Manchka, who headed the I.D.'s sub-Saharan section from 1970 to 1978, when Soviet involvement escalated so dramatically, was also removed, so the globalists are in the ascendant and the Africanists in decline.

The I.D. has three sections for African policy. The one for southern Africa, created in the 1970s, is headed by Andrei I. Urnov, whose writings on Africa are also extensive.[10] Below the three deputies and Urnov are analysts for specific countries (some are responsible for more than one country). For example, Vladimir I. Shubin heads the South Africa Department, and Eduard A. Kapskiy has been responsible for Mozambique and Sao Tome and Principe since 1980. Boris I. Petruk has been responsible for Angola and Ethiopia since 1982. The I.D. also uses consultants and journalists like Viktor I. Sidenko and Veniamin A. Midtsev.

The Foreign Ministry's Southern African Apparatus

The Foreign Ministry also has three sections for Africa. One is responsible for eastern and southern Africa because the South African insurgents have camps at Mzimbu in Tanzania, East Africa. The head of this section is Vladlen I. Vasev. He supervises country desk officers like Ivan A. Gogitze, a Georgian responsible for the Republic of South Africa. During the 1988 peace talks among Cuba, South Africa, and Angola, Vasev was frequently present.

Gorbachev's reorganization of the Foreign Ministry reflects Africa's importance. He created three deputy ministers for Africa instead of one. He also created a special African Countries Administration within the ministry headed by Yuri Yukalov, a former ambassador and counselor in Tanzania, where the African National Congress (ANC) has always maintained a strong presence.

One deputy foreign minister, Anatoly L. Adamishin, who has traveled widely throughout the region, is a West Europeanist, reflecting the more global orientation of Soviet policy toward the region. He consulted with the U.S. mediator of the 1988 peace talks for Namibia and Angola before and after most sessions.

Like the I.D., the Foreign Ministry has desk officers responsible for specific countries, but unlike the I.D., the ministry has agents in the field—that is, it has embassies. The staffs of these southern African embassies are expanding rapidly, and new embassies are being established.[11]

The first ambassador in the newly established Lesotho embassy, Vladimir I. Gavryushkin, had been previously expelled from both the London and the Ottawa embassies for espionage, so he was presumably a KGB professional, as was the former ambassador to Zambia (1981–1985), Vladimir A. Cherednik, expelled from both Kenya and Ghana for espionage. The Soviet ambassador to Botswana, Nicolai I. Petrov, was also a professional intelligence operative who was expelled from Kenya in 1967, Ghana in 1971, and Mali in 1978.

In 1988 a new ambassador, Boris A. Asoyan, arrived in Lesotho. He is an academic, a journalist, and former deputy director of the Africa Institute and has served on the staff of both the Central Committee of the party and the Foreign Ministry. After a short, but active, stay in Lesotho, he returned to Moscow to assume the position of deputy chief in the Second Africa Department of the Foreign Ministry.

A. I. Kalinin has been ambassador to Angola since 1985, but unlike N. K. Dybenko, the ambassador to Mozambique, he was not a member of the CPSU Central Committee. In fact, Dybenko is the only ambassador in the region holding this high party post.[12]

In 1984 and 1985 Soviet embassies in southern Africa more than tripled their staffs in many cases, with virtually all the new arrivals being suspected intelligence or military personnel.[13] The Mozambique embassy went from 35 to 100, the Zimbabwe embassy from 17 to 65, and the Botswana embassy from 21 to 60 (see table 1). In tiny, landlocked Lesotho with no Soviet residents or trade, a new embassy was established with a staff of approximately 27.

Fronts and Academic Exchanges: Disinformation and Public Diplomacy

Although the I.D., the Foreign Ministry, and the KGB are the Politburo's major sources of information on southern Africa, other important sources include the Committee for Solidarity with the Peoples of Asia and Africa, which serves as host to visiting leaders and as a channel for funds to insurgencies like SWAPO, the ANC, or, before independence, the Popular Movement for the Liberation of Angola (MPLA). The committee's head is Mirza I. Ibragimov, apparently a theoretician and ideologue. His deputy, Vasily G. Solodovnikov, was ambassador to Zambia and was demoted for not backing the successful insurgents who took power in Zimbabwe in 1980, the most dramatic Soviet miscalculation in southern Africa. In 1988 Solodov-

TABLE 1
EXPANSION OF SOUTHERN AFRICAN EMBASSY STAFFS

	1983	1985
Mozambique	35	100
Zimbabwe	17	65
Botswana	21	60
Lesotho	0	27

SOURCE: *Foreign Broadcast Information Services,* October 1985

nikov met a group of South Africans, including important Afrikaners, in East Germany. Ibragimov's predecessor was Rostislav Ulyanovsky, the former deputy I.D. chief, which suggests that the I.D. and the committee work together closely.

The other important source of specifically African information is the Africa Institute, although its scholars seldom actually go to Africa, unlike delegations of the Committee for Solidarity with the Peoples of Asia and Africa. Headed by former Americanist Anatoly A. Gromyko, the institute has had a formidable staff, including deputy directors such as Gleb I. Starushenko, Aleksandr I. Vasiliyev, Igor A. Belayev, Leonard V. Goncharov, and Boris A. Asoyan, who later became ambassador to Lesotho and then deputy foreign minister. All of them comment widely on southern Africa in the Soviet media and at international scholarly conferences, where they presumably pick up valuable information.

Goncharov, a deputy director of the Africa Institute, did travel to Zimbabwe in June 1987 to deliver a paper in which he argued that the USSR would not seek to interfere in a postrevolutionary South African settlement.[14] This contradicted a paper given by Starushenko in Moscow a year before wherein he appeared to interfere by advising the ANC to propose a bill of rights to be implemented when it seized power. Starushenko's paper was widely interpreted as announcing a less hostile policy toward the present government of the Republic of South Africa, but a careful reading reveals a proposal designed to advance Moscow's interests by dividing the ruling class.[15] In addition, some Soviet academics visited the region in mid-1989 and served a public diplomacy function as well as an information-gathering one.

Although Soviet academics can visit the region, they are banned from the Republic of South Africa itself. Nevertheless, South African academics and journalists are meeting their Soviet counterparts in adjacent countries and in the USSR.[16] As mentioned previously, when Boris A. Asoyan, formerly an analyst with the Africa Institute, was appointed ambassador to Lesotho, a major new Soviet listening post, he met numerous South African academics.[17]

After his brief stay in Lesotho, Asoyan emerged as deputy chief of the Foreign Ministry's Second Africa Department. His writings, less Marxist and more pragmatic, reflect a more informed Soviet assessment of South African realities, as well as some ambivalence, just as there is greater ambivalence on other major issues. An example of this non-Marxist analysis is Asoyan's blaming the Calvinists, not the capitalists, for apartheid.

In late 1988 the South African government itself quietly hosted a Soviet journalist, and in 1989 Yuri Yakalov, head of the Foreign Ministry's African Affairs Division, met with leading Afrikaner intellectuals and a former head of the Broederbond in London. (The Broederbond is a secret society of Afrikaner leaders that has significantly influenced government policy since 1978, when the National party took power; it reportedly has more influence with F. W. de Klerk than it did with P. W. Botha.)

Some South Africans are also visiting the USSR despite the absence of diplomatic relations, providing another source of information for the Soviets. In the fall of 1987, Goncharov conferred in Moscow at the Africa Institute with a leading Afrikaner expert on the USSR, Philip Nel, head of the newly created Institute for Soviet Studies at Stellenbosch, the premier Afrikaner university. In November 1988 two analysts from the South African Institute of Race Relations interviewed numerous Soviet Africanists in Moscow and discovered considerable differences over policy, but they concluded that the closer these people were to official circles, the more they stressed the basic continuity of Soviet policy.[18] These contacts, which constitute much more than an information-gathering exercise, represent a public diplomacy offensive designed to portray the USSR as reasonable and pragmatic and to open new channels of influence. They also are used to encourage divisions in a white society that has always been virulently anti-communist.

Some Soviet academics are involved in what amounts to espionage. For example, Anatoly A. Gromyko, head of the Africa Institute, privately asked the British whether they would back the transfer of sensitive technology to the Republic of South Africa. There, the KGB could acquire it because the republic is not part of the Coordinating Committee for Multilateral Export Controls (CoCom), which regulates such transfers to the USSR and other communist countries.[19] As we shall see, the KGB has used South Africa for these purposes.

TABLE 2
EMBASSY STAFFS AND INTELLIGENCE OPERATIVES (1986)

	Diplomats	Intelligence Operatives
Botswana	25	28
Zambia	54	75
Zimbabwe	40	22

SOURCE: William Pascoe, "Moscow's Strategy in Southern Africa," *The Backgrounder*, July 21, 1986.

KGB: Espionage and Disinformation

That the Republic of South Africa is the centerpiece of KGB activity in southern Africa is suggested by three major spy scandals spanning almost two decades. But KGB activity is pervasive throughout the entire region. As mentioned before, the former ambassadors to Lesotho and Zambia were expelled from two previous embassy postings for espionage, which means they are probably KGB operatives. There is some evidence that a KGB professional, Vasily G. Solodovnikov, coordinated Soviet policy through the region during the 1970s from his ostensible post as ambassador to Zambia. In 1988 he resurfaced in West Germany as host to a group of South Africans, including ANC and Afrikaner delegates. In any case, the KGB has certainly been involved in many activities in the region for a long time (see table 2).[20]

In 1982 and 1983, American and British intelligence unmasked a high-ranking South African naval officer, Commodore Dieter Gebhardt, who had worked for the KGB for more than twenty years and according to his superiors "knew everything." Gebhardt had visited Moscow five times and apparently revealed the most sensitive security data on South Africa to his superiors, including the capabilities of the major naval bases, the magnitude of fuel storage facilities, the activities of the naval electronic monitoring systems for ships rounding the Cape of Good Hope, and presumably the state of the South African nuclear development program. In addition, Gebhardt made available details of British naval maneuvers during the Falklands crisis and the details of both South American and Western military and intelligence cooperation with South Africa.

Going further, Gebhardt helped facilitate an elaborate scheme to acquire sophisticated U.S. electronic and computer equipment for the USSR. American computers and electronic equipment were shipped through South Africa to Sweden and then to the USSR with Gebhardt's help.

The second spy scandal occurred in 1967 when the South Africans arrested and convicted a KGB operative, Yuri Loginov, alias Edmund Trinka, who had served Soviet intelligence in Egypt. An important operative, he spoke fluent English with an American accent and was trained for three occupations—travel writer, welder, and bookkeeper. Loginov provided information on Soviet clandestine activities in 23 countries before being exchanged for West German agents held by the USSR. The evidence suggests that his primary concern was the state of development of the South African nuclear program.

The third major spy scandal in South Africa surfaced in 1981, with the arrest of another KGB operative, Major Alexei Kozlov, whose primary mission was to assess the political situation in Namibia and South Africa, particularly the effectiveness of the insurgents in both countries. He reportedly found neither to be very impressive. He concluded that the ANC had not taken advantage of the 1976 uprisings in Soweto, a Johannesburg suburb, and that SWAPO could not win an election in Namibia unless it indulged in widespread intimidation. He also concluded that the ANC was wasting the financial aid provided by the Kremlin. That Kozlov was a significant KGB operative is again reflected in the spy exchange that returned him to Moscow: the Soviets traded eight "important" Western agents for Kozlov.

Perhaps most interesting about Kozlov's case is the mixed bag of information made available to the Soviets. Kozlov correctly assessed the prospects for revolution in South Africa, which were nil, but his evaluation of SWAPO's influence is less impressive, for SWAPO's popularity was widespread. Thus the Soviet decision-making process was not well served by what should have been one of its best sources. Ironically, Soviet African specialists at the time were describing South Africa as a volcano that could be expected to erupt any minute, adding this contradictory assessment by academics to the inaccurate information supplied by the KGB. When expert information is repeatedly misleading, decision makers often resort to their personal prejudices and preconceptions, which may account for some of Moscow's miscalculations in the region.

The other interesting element of the Kozlov episode is the apparent friction between the KGB on the one hand and the insurgents on the other. This is not the only case of African-Soviet friction. Soviet military advisers frequently quarreled with officers in the armies in Angola and Mozambique. Also, the *African Communist,* organ of the South African Communist Party (SACP), expresses a lack of enthusiasm about *glasnost'* in Aesopian language.

The size and character of KGB activity in this area, far from the Soviet periphery, reflects Moscow's concern for fashioning a policy that can enhance its influence worldwide, not just in this region.

Although no Soviet diplomat has officially set foot in South Africa since the USSR and the Republic of South Africa severed relations in 1956, the KGB remains active in the region, not only to inform the Soviet leadership but also to misinform the world. The KGB is a major instrument of Soviet public diplomacy, which includes disinformation as well as dissemination. In its propaganda department, the biggest section has been the one for southern Africa. The KGB works through a myriad of fronts and contacts to manipulate the unpopularity of the South African political system and its alleged close ties with the United States.[21]

Three examples of the role of disinformation in Soviet public diplomacy for southern Africa surfaced in Zimbabwe in 1983 and 1984. All were printed by the country's leading newspaper, the *Herald,* and were completely false. All of course were designed to portray the United States and South Africa as military and political allies.

In December 1983 the *Herald* reported a plan to test and deploy U.S. cruise missiles in South Africa. This was later revealed to be a Soviet disinformation scheme, a complete hoax, which the *Herald* ultimately disclaimed.[22]

Several months later the *Herald* again succumbed to Soviet disinformation when it reported that the United States recruited helicopter pilots to serve in the South African military. At the same time it also reported that the United States had offered to sell F-5 fighters to the South African Air Force in violation of the 1963 U.N. arms embargo. The stories were based on documents forged by the KGB. These episodes reflect one of the central tactics of Moscow's strategy for southern Africa: using the crisis there to discredit the United States throughout the world.

That such incredible stories could be printed by one of the best newspapers in this region demonstrates the opportunities available to the Kremlin there, but the crudeness of the scheme and its unmasking illustrate that Soviet tactics can often be counterproductive in the long run.

Because South Africa was a mainstay of the Union for the Total Independence of Angola's (UNITA's) insurgency against the Soviet-backed MPLA that rules Angola, any news about that nation tended to include the alleged U.S.–South African alliance line.[23] The credibility of such news is enhanced by the fact that the United States provides covert support for UNITA (this aid was designed to decrease South African influence over UNITA). That the U.S. Congress by an overwhelming vote invoked sanctions against South Africa is also conveniently ignored. Nevertheless, an increasing awareness and understanding of these facts is gradually attenuating the impact of Moscow's public diplomacy offensive.

The simplemindedness and inaccuracy of this U.S.–South African collusion theme is gradually being appreciated by some Soviets. In early 1988 Moscow's ambassador to Lesotho characterized the accepted global image of South Africa as "a caricature, not a living image of a multifaceted, dynamic, extremely complex and confused reality."[24]

The Salience of Public Diplomacy

Sophistication and an emphasis on public diplomacy have emerged as hallmarks of Soviet foreign policy under Mikhail Gorbachev, who began his career in the propaganda organ of the party. One of his first acts as CPSU leader was to reorganize the propaganda apparatus, and in 1987 the party secretary responsible for propaganda, Alexander N. Yakovlev, was promoted to the ruling Politburo. In 1988 Yakovlev assumed the chairmanship of the Foreign Policy Commission. He has lived and studied in the West and has a reputation for being fiercely anti-American. He is an expert on the West and an advocate of a public diplomacy strategy that will extract advantages for the Kremlin from the international political vulnerabilities of the United States by aggravating latent anti-American sentiment.[25] One such vulnerability is the widespread misperception that the United States supports South Africa's racial policies, despite their universal condemnation throughout the country.

Some time ago, Thomas Henriksen astutely noted that in South Africa "the Western nations find their strategic and material self-interest in conflict with their beliefs and practices of racial democracy."[26] The Politburo's leading specialist on public diplomacy, Alexander Yakovlev, seems to have persuaded Gorbachev to exploit this dilemma.

In a similar vein, Karen Brutents, the first deputy head of the CPSU International Department, has emphasized the anti-imperialism—in other words, anti–United States—theme in his writings, calling especially for a new stress on contacts with noncommunist, but anti-imperialist, states.[27] In late 1988 the USSR seemed to be preparing to harvest some of the growing anti-American sentiment in South Africa, when a Soviet journalist accepted an invitation from the South African government to tour that country.[28] That this was in any way a precursor to diplomatic recognition, however, has been vehemently denied.[29] The USSR sought to have it both ways by taking advantage of anti-American sentiment while projecting its image as the bulwark of the anti-apartheid movement.

There is certainly genuine disagreement within the Soviet establishment among other reasons because foreign aid is unpopular and because ethnic Russian nationalism may be somewhat sympathetic with Afrikaner nationalism.

Throughout 1988 and 1989 a second theme of Soviet public diplomacy re-emerged: the coequal status of the USSR and the United States as global superpowers. As a series of meetings between the superpowers on southern Africa at the ministerial, ambassadorial, and expert levels progressed, the coequality theme, long a staple of Soviet policy, surfaced more frequently. Cooperation with the United States over this far-flung area of the world demonstrated Moscow's "legitimate" concerns in every corner of the globe. The Kremlin's participation—as an observer in the Namibia-Angola talks, with the United States as broker—was portrayed as a reflection of this parity between superpowers; Moscow maintained its anti-imperialism stance by refusing to sit at the table with South Africa. As an even more specific symbol of parity, the December 1988 accords for Namibia and Angola invited the United States and the USSR to serve jointly as observers on the commission to verify and monitor the implementation of the peace process.[30]

Conclusion: Low-Risk Globalism and Public Diplomacy

Soviet behavior and the nature and composition of the southern African decision-making apparatus suggest a long-range strategy for the region, perhaps best characterized as low-risk globalism, in which public diplomacy plays a central role. As the head of the Africa Department of the Foreign Ministry put it in 1989: "We intend to establish the most intensive contacts with the press, the media as a whole, and the public."[31] Soviet public diplomacy toward this region has emphasized two themes over the years. The parity theme is highlighted when Moscow seeks some accommodation to advance its interests, but the theme of portraying the United States as the bulwark of imperialism and the USSR as the bulwark of the progressive forces has always been paramount.

2

SOUTH AFRICA

*Armed Struggle,
Diplomacy,
and Duplicity*

Soviet policy toward South Africa stresses support for the insurgent ANC, which has been publicly allied with the SACP for decades.[1] The SACP is the Kremlin's key instrument in South Africa and is the classic, small, elite intellectual vanguard party (see table 3). The ANC is also enmeshed in a complex network of pro-Soviet front organizations.[2]

Theoretically, the Marxist-Leninist worldview is more appropriate for the Republic of South Africa than for the adjacent Afro-Marxist states, whose cultures are more peasant and tribal. South Africa does have a large urbanized industrial proletariat and is more developed than most African states. It is also somewhat more detribalized, although the subtle strength of ethnic ties can be easily underestimated.

After the unrest in the mid-1980s, Moscow was less sanguine about an imminent revolution and began pursuing other avenues of influence. It also directed the SACP to concentrate more on political tactics. In addition, other somewhat duplicitous facets of Soviet policy began to play an increasing role in Moscow's quest for influence in that country.

TABLE 3
POLITBURO OF SOUTH AFRICAN COMMUNIST PARTY, 1988
(ELECTED IN 1984 AT MOSCOW CONGRESS)

Dan Tloome	chairman
Joe Slovo	secretary general
Chris Hani	chief of staff of the military wing
Ray Simons	labor theoretician, uses pen name R. S. Nyameko
Mac Maharaj	political strategist, directs recruitment inside South Africa
Thabo Mbeki	information chief
John Nkadimeng	general secretary of SACTU, the banned labor union

SOURCE: *Africa Confidential* 29, no. 17, August 26, 1988, p. 4.

Gorbachev's Long-Range Strategy for South Africa

Mikhail Gorbachev's long-range policy, as reflected in Moscow's behavior and rhetoric, is two-pronged: multifaceted diplomacy combined with a carefully orchestrated, low-intensity campaign of sabotage and subversion, usually referred to as armed propaganda by the ANC.

To some extent, Moscow was unprepared for the unrest in South Africa's townships in 1984–1985, with young radicals calling spontaneously for revolutionary activity without guidance from the Kremlin. Gorbachev came to power as the violence peaked, but his regime was not long in unveiling its long-range strategy with a new tactical focus: emphasizing political alliances with opponents of the regime, reminiscent of the popular front strategy of Stalin.

In summary, by the summer of 1988, after the success of the South African security forces in quelling the unrest, Moscow had shifted its revolutionary strategy to the long haul. The new stress was on political stratagems designed to divide the ruling class and unite the opposition rather than on premature violence, which arguably might unite the ruling class against the insurgents. This new emphasis has had limited success. There have been major inroads in the unions, but this may have stimulated a reaction. Some of the liberal opposition has talked of uniting and cooperating with the ANC, but has failed to do so. Finally and most significantly, radicals in the ANC are gradually assuming positions of real authority and are clearly reluctant to follow Moscow's lead, preferring a greater emphasis on violence. Talented young SACP members, however, are emerging to harness the violence to an overall political strategy, although the SACP is still probably run in the main by aging cadres, like Joe Slovo, who live in exile.

Moscow Announces a Popular Front Strategy

In July 1987 *Pravda* explicitly noted the divisions among whites and called for an alliance between opposition groups against the South African regime. "The time is coming to break down the barriers. The more people who have a hand in this, the more quickly will come the hour of freedom," the article commented.[3] A month later on Moscow radio the SACP's long-standing leader, Joe Slovo, exulted in the fragmentation of the ruling class and the "great benefit to the liberation struggle" of this development.[4]

All this was foreshadowed in a paper by Gleb Starushenko, a deputy director of the African Institute, delivered in Moscow in June 1986 that called for a bill of rights as a device for dividing the ruling class and facilitating revolution: "Already today the ANC might work out comprehensive guarantees for the White population which could be implemented after the elimination of the regime of apartheid. Such guarantees would suit both the liberals and the pragmatists from the White community, neutralizing at the same time the diehards."[5] The whites are already divided over the question of how much an ANC government could be trusted to implement a bill of rights.

The chief purpose of this strategy is to build alliances with black and white groups opposed to the government.[6] A corollary is that this would divide the white ruling class and facilitate revolution. In 1988 the second deputy chief of the African Department of the Foreign Ministry, Boris Asoyan, put it this way:

> It is safe to state that the revolution in South Africa is already going on . . . [V]ictory of the anti-apartheid movement is most probable.
>
> Even larger segments break away from the "white tribe" segments which, even if not going over to the opposed camp, become enemies of the ideology and policy of the ruling minority. The allies of the liberation force, voluntary or not, from among intellectuals, businessmen, religious leaders, and the youth are growing in number every day.[7]

The ANC style of work and its rhetoric are essentially, though not completely, Leninist.[8] According to the classic Leninist revolutionary strategy, the SACP would infiltrate the ANC, which would then penetrate other groups, forming a popular front for overthrowing the regime. In the second stage the SACP would seize power. This is the so-called two-stage revolutionary process.

From the beginning of their alliance in 1962, the ANC and SACP accepted this two-stage process as an overall framework for their relationship. In the first stage, the SACP would help the ANC, as the leading force, to overthrow the regime, and then in the second stage it would work to establish a communist government.[9] There is more to Soviet strategy than this—as discussed further on—but because this is the central thrust of Moscow's policy, let's examine how well it has worked.

Penetrating the Unions: A Significant Success

The new Soviet approach has had some success in the unions and to a lesser extent among white liberals. The most important development has been SACP's establishment of significant influence inside South Africa's largest union, the 500,000-member Congress of South African Trade Unions (COSATU).[10] Viewing itself as the political vanguard of the working class, the SACP has worked hard since 1984, when it held its sixth congress in Moscow, to penetrate the union membership, most of whom originally eschewed politics for economic gains.

To put this in perspective, South African trade unions operate within an economy marked by heavy unemployment. No more than 10 percent of the African labor force is unionized, and striking workers can be replaced to some extent by migrant labor from neighboring states like Mozambique and Lesotho.

The labor or economics-first element is still probably the majority in most unions. But in COSATU the populist, that is, the politically oriented, pro-SACP element is very strong, if not a majority. Allied with COSATU is the six hundred–plus United Democratic Front (UDF), a coalition of "civic" groups that poses the largest opposition to the government; its penetration by SACP therefore represents a significant victory for Gorbachev's new strategy of seeking to promote ANC alliances with all opposition groups.

Penetrating the White Opposition: Limited Success

Even the most restrained acts of sabotage alienate the white liberals, retarding, if not completely foreclosing, any significant cooperation, much less an alliance. Thus Moscow and the ANC confront a dilemma: how can they reach out to the white opposition while conducting a campaign of violent subversion, especially when ANC radicals advocate and carry out violent acts that may go beyond anything acceptable to Moscow or even the top ANC leaders?

The evidence suggests that these radicals increasingly occupy positions that influence policy. The statements of Chris Hani, military chief of staff, and Steve Tswete—two SACP members elected to the ANC's ruling National Executive Council (NEC) in July 1988—reflect the views of the militants regarding diminishing concern for civilian casualties. Tswete was removed as head of political commissars, but he was promoted to the NEC in July 1988, suggesting an ongoing struggle over military policy. Tswete had just fled South Africa and had gone to East Germany for two months' training.[11]

Although claiming that only military, police, and paramilitary objectives are targeted, Tswete commented: "But there has to be an element of *terror* of ruthlessness, for the struggle to have effect [emphasis added]."[12] In July 1988 a bomb went off in Johannesburg with nothing but rugby fans in the area. Bishop Desmond Tutu, an important ANC ally, condemned this action, illustrating Moscow's dilemma. The bomb was much larger and more sophisticated than the usual limpet mine, indicating according to Tom Lodge, that ANC headquarters authorized this attack on civilians.[13]

The slow but steady evolution of ANC strategy toward a classic terrorism is reflected in an ANC telex to foreign correspondents in Johannesburg after the July 1988 rugby bombings. The telex read (*Baltimore Sun*, August 18, 1988, p. 7): "It is contrary to our policy to select targets whose *sole* objective is to strike at civilians" [emphasis added]. Although interpreted by ANC sympathizers as the nearest thing an apology yet offered for a bombing, in fact it implied that a major—if not the sole—objective of bombings is civilian. This classic terrorist strategy is designed to create a pervasive climate of fear in a society because of the sheer horror of deliberately killing innocent civilians.

With respect to the white liberals, although the ANC alliance strategy conflicts with its campaign of violence, the alliance tactics are interesting. The essential objective—an old staple of Leninism—is to divide the ruling class, the whites. Marxist-Leninist theoreticians do not see all whites as members of the ruling class; more than 80 percent depend on salaries and wages and don't own the means of production.

The whites have been considerably divided for some time, but Soviet and ANC strategy seeks to encourage the white opposition to unite against the regime, or at least coordinate its efforts with the ANC.

In fact, at a secret meeting in Frankfurt in spring 1988, ANC leaders encouraged white liberals to unite inside and outside parliament and for the first time supported a multiparty democracy as a device to lure the liberals into a tacit alliance. Because some important liberals were not present, the viability of the strategy, particularly if it is perceived by the liberals as an integral part of a violent revolutionary strategy, is questionable.

Those present at the Frankfurt meeting made no commitments, but the secret multiparty proposal reflects a divide-and-conquer strategy, especially because the ANC refused to commit itself to participation in scheduled elections inside South Africa.[14] In the summer of 1988 the ANC hinted that it might unveil a constitution along these lines[15] by circulating a set of guidelines for a future constitution aimed at attracting liberal and union support. It called for a bill of rights, an independent judiciary, and the right to strike. The chairman of the drafting committee was Ray Simons, a veteran Communist. Simons is on the SACP Politburo and writes under the pen name R. S. Nyameko for the SACP organ, the *African Communist*. The key figure in drafting the bill of rights was Albie Sachs, another veteran Communist.[16]

This alliance strategy is also designed to keep white liberals at odds with the ruling National party, thus weakening the regime politically. For example, according to ANC officials, the constitutional guidelines would ban the ruling National party.

For some time, Soviets have been seeking to influence Afrikaners as well as English-speaking liberals, perhaps hoping to wean them away from the ruling party and thus weaken it further. Radio Moscow began regular Afrikaans broadcasts in the mid-1980s. A few prominent Afrikaners had already rejected the Nationalist party and moved to parties on its left, not just its right. In October 1988, the ANC and the Soviets sat down for discussions in West Germany with a group of white liberals, including former officials of the Botha government, as well as Afrikaners and English with well-known left leanings. The Soviet delegation was led by Vasily Solodovnikov, former ambassador to Zambia, who coordinated Soviet policy during the Rhodesian rebellion. Now vice-chairman of the Soviet Afro-Asian Solidarity Committee, his re-emergence reflects the essential continuity of Soviet strategy.[17]

Nevertheless, a strategy of revolutionary violence is clearly ANC policy. A major policy statement issued in Lusaka, Zambia, in February 1988 explicitly spells this out: "Vindicate our often-repeated conviction that only a mass movement, uniting in its ranks the broadest front of democratic and patriotic forces and employing a multipronged strategy that includes revolutionary violence, can dislodge the apartheid regime."[18]

The relative conformity of ANC and Soviet strategy is reflected in a June 1988 lecture by Boris Asoyan, then Soviet ambassador to Lesotho and now deputy chief of the Foreign Ministry's Africa Department:

> We accept the necessity of the stage-by-stage movement to the main aim, creation of a nonracial democratic society, and concede that negotiations between the government and the genuine representatives of the black majority will be a necessary and inevitable link in this process.
>
> At the same time I am sure that the power of pressure on Pretoria, *including armed struggle by the liberation organizations, is also an indispensable part of this process.* So is the demand for sanctions [emphasis added].[19]

Because *any* violence alienates the liberals, whom the Soviets and the ANC are courting, a policy involving armed struggle poses a dilemma.

Statements of Soviet officials implying that the armed struggle should not be expanded and that South Africa should not be destroyed ameliorate this. But there is no way of resolving this dilemma as long as the ANC refuses to abandon its policy of armed struggle. Moscow, the SACP, and the ANC can, however, continue to publicly repudiate a policy that injures innocent civilians by excusing specific incidents as unauthorized or the work of the most militant radicals. It is a fig leaf, but it is the best that can be done, given the internal contradictions of the strategy.

Many in the ANC, especially among the older generation, must abhor such behavior, and Lenin himself considered it counterproductive at this stage of revolutionary preparation. But from a public diplomacy viewpoint, it does tend to draw world attention to the inequities within the society and the alleged progressive role of the Soviets. Gorbachev's sophisticated public diplomacy advisers must see this as the best that can be hoped for in an enormously complex situation.

If repression escalates, then radical influence is likely to do so also. Although for the time being this represents a constraint on Soviet policy, in the long run, Moscow, as the ANC's chief supplier of arms, is increasingly likely to assert its authority through the SACP over even the ANC's most militant elements. The new Soviet pragmatism has mitigated the rigid ideologically pre-Gorbachevite SACP, but its dependence on the USSR for military and financial assistance is almost total. Friction over the degree of socialism in a post-apartheid regime and the extent to which violence can be employed effectively are unlikely to weaken Moscow's influence significantly. Thus without substantial reform, time favors the low-intensity Soviet approach.

Military Aid and Training

Although the Soviets often deny it, since 1969 most of the ANC's military and financial aid has come from the USSR and its allies. The USSR funnels most aid to the ANC through the liberation committee of the Organization of African Unity (OAU), which is why Soviet Foreign Ministry spokesman Yuri Afanasyev could claim in May 1986 that "the Soviet Union gave no military assistance to the ANC."[20] Thus the USSR can deny responsibility where convenient while ingratiating itself with much of African public opinion.

Nevertheless, after his November 1986 meeting with Gorbachev, ANC president Oliver Tambo said his request for more military assistance was granted "as usual."[21] Going further, he said "the Soviet Union is resolved to contribute everything within its possibilities."[22] In 1987 Tambo said the USSR gave the ANC £24 million per year. In 1962 Soviet aid amounted to a paltry £1 million by comparison.[23] But the ANC's military achievements have been scanty, despite all this help.

In 1982 the U.S. State Department estimated that the ANC received approximately 60 percent of its financial support, 90 percent of its arms, and most of its military training from the USSR, East Germany, and Cuba.[24] This dependence may diminish if, as rumored, substantial Nigerian and Chinese assistance materializes, but the extensive attention given by the Soviet media to the ANC's 75th anniversary in January 1987 and the establishment of a new ANC office in Moscow suggest an increasing Soviet commitment.[25] Scandinavia, especially Sweden (which gives an estimated $20 million per year in cash), has always provided nonmilitary aid.[26]

Until 1989, when it was forced to move to Tanzania, Uganda, and Ethiopia, the ANC received military training primarily in Angola at Viana, Quibaxe, and elsewhere under Cuban and East German instructors. The training in Angola's Benguela region included the use of 82-mm mortars, 75-mm cannon, and bayonets, as well as training in sabotage, guerrilla tactics, and theory.[27] Until recently ANC equipment was unsophisticated, but in 1988 the ANC claimed to be supplying the SAM-7 to its cells inside South Africa.[28]

Some advanced training takes place in the USSR, Eastern Europe, and Cuba. For example, at one camp, Provoloye in the Ukraine, there are courses on artillery, anti-aircraft, and guerrilla operations. There is also a training facility at the well-known Center 26 near Moscow.[29] At this center one ANC defector claims to have undergone ten months of training for organizing ten-person cells for political agitation after being infiltrated into South Africa.[30] He also went to Marxist Mozambique for lectures on political strategy.[31] One estimate suggests that about twenty people a month leave for insurgency training.[32] The comings and goings of insurgents from these camps are occasionally reported in the international press.[33]

ANC sources say each guerrilla is taught to train four new insurgents inside South Africa, and these new trainees then train four more.[34] The major infiltration route now is probably through Zimbabwe, where "it's very easy to cross ... to South Africa," according to a Zimbabwean minister. Normally an ANC guerrilla unit has AK-47 assault rifles, explosives, and hand grenades, almost all of Soviet, East German, or Czech origin. Inside South Africa, ANC cells of five to ten people house and feed the infiltrators. Because no cell knows the identity of members of other cells, the number of cells is difficult to determine. The state of emergency in South Africa, cross-border raids by South African commandos, and the insurgencies in Angola by UNITA and in Mozambique by the Mozambique National Resistance probably have slowed infiltration and training significantly.

South African police experts on the ANC claim that it has no infrastructure in South Africa at all and that only 30 trained people are active inside the country.[35] In 1983, U.S. intelligence concluded that there were from one to two thousand insurgents inside the country.[36] The South African figure is undoubtedly low because Alan Cowell of the *New York Times* reported seeing what amounted to an infrastructure in June 1986. The ANC was training young radicals in the segregated South African townships in the use of explosives.[37]

Estimates of the number of trained insurgents both inside and outside South Africa vary from below six thousand to ten thousand. This is up from an estimated four thousand in 1978. A source close to the ANC put the number at seven thousand.[38]

The Military Arm: *Umkhonto we Sizwe*. Although the USSR's influence in the ANC's military wing—*Umkhonto we Sizwe,* which means "spear of the nation" in the Zulu language—is substantial for obvious reasons, there has been considerable friction between East bloc instructors and ANC trainees. Moscow has a well-known disdain for African insurgents, which exacerbates relations between patron and client.[39]

This disdain emanates from the ANC's poor security and its inability so far to carry out sabotage on a large scale. The disdain is aggravated by a mistaken perception among many Soviets that aid to liberation movements causes shortages in the USSR, as well as by the resentment of privileges accorded African students and trainees in the Soviet Union.

The ANC's faulty security situation was highlighted in 1986 when a South African agent in the SACP, Glory Lephosha Sidebe, alias Comrade September, exposed ANC activities in Swaziland. This led to the death of Cassius Make, the ANC's chief of ordnance, and the abduction of the local ANC branch chief.

Joe Slovo, a founder and key military strategist for *Umkhonto* and a veteran Communist, was promoted in 1985 to the ANC's ruling National Executive Council. But most authorities think the military commander in chief, Joe Modise, is not a Communist. Modise is not only the commander but also chairs the Military Committee, which plans military policy, subject to approval by the entire NEC.[40] However, his chief of staff, Chris Hani, who was elevated to the NEC in July 1988, is reportedly on the Politburo of the SACP. Josiah Jele, the executive secretary of the Political Military Council (PMC), which coordinates the armed struggle and underground activity inside South Africa, is also an SACP member and close to Modise personally.

Nevertheless, Slovo is usually credited with a major role in planning military policy and is often characterized as a KGB agent, although he denies it.[41] As secretary general of the SACP, he is close to the Soviets and probably the most reliable instrument of Soviet policy in the ANC leadership.

The transfer of Slovo in early 1987 from the position of SACP chairman to the lesser post of secretary general and his resignation as *Umkhonto* chief of staff suggest the ANC is seeking to moderate its image as its leaders reach out to the West in such meetings as those with former Secretary of State George Shultz and lower-ranking British and U.S. officials. Some suggest that the post of secretary general has been downgraded because it remained vacant for a year after the death of the previous occupant, Moses Mabhida. But this is unlikely, given the importance of such posts in all communist organizations.[42] The position of chairman is usually an honorary post in communist parties like this.

Slovo is still on the NEC and the PMC, where he is likely to continue to exercise considerable influence over political and military policy. But his authority may be threatened by the more radical Chris Hani, who is reportedly a Communist and supported by five members of the eight-person *Umkhonto* high command.[43] A disagreement over bombing strategy apparently extends to the SACP as well as to the ANC.

Diplomacy and Duplicity: Gorbachev's Multifaceted Strategy

There is more to Gorbachev's strategy than the SACP connection and military aid. The Soviets are conducting a diplomatic offensive and urging the ANC to do likewise. Moscow is prodding the ANC to broaden its international contacts and its alliances with black groups inside South Africa.

Although only the USSR, East Germany, and Romania have recognized the ANC as the authentic representative of the South African people, it has partial diplomatic status in 26 capitals, mostly in the West. The Soviets are encouraging the ANC to approach countries like India and the frontline states, as well as to reach out to other black organizations in South Africa itself, like the Pan-African Congress (PAC).[44]

More important, Moscow is quietly approaching the Americans and hinting in public about joint Soviet-U.S. initiatives to resolve regional difficulties.[45] This represents a diplomatic effort to insert the USSR even further into an area historically under Western hegemony. It is also designed to project an image of parity between superpowers that can intervene anywhere on the globe.

Moscow, of course, apparently did not object either to the Nkomati Accords or to the Namibia-Angola Accords, which removed ANC military facilities from Mozambique and Angola and implicitly from Namibia.

Moscow is even meeting secretly with South African officials, an act of duplicity from the ANC's perspective, that suggests the Kremlin is anticipating more than one outcome. According to the South African government, senior Soviet officials contacted rather low-level South African officials in 1987.[46] But in 1989 Deputy Foreign Minister Anatoly Adamishin met secretly with high-level government officials in South Africa. Although such approaches may signal a genuine desire for dialogue, they may also represent an effort to manipulate the regime and lull it into a false sense of security. Such duplicity has been a hallmark of Soviet diplomacy in the past.

The Soviets are keeping their options open, hoping to enhance their influence whatever happens in South Africa. This can hardly endear them to the ANC.

One Soviet analyst has even called for a constitution that would include classification by racial group in the upper house, a proposal roundly condemned by the ANC, causing somewhat of a temporary backlash against the USSR, according to the Soviets themselves.[47] In short, the USSR is supporting an insurgency while touching base with most elements of a potential future confederation, and increasingly carrying on semicovert diplomatic and economic relations with the government it is trying to overthrow—not unfamiliar behavior in the history of Soviet foreign policy.

After the shuffle of ANC personnel in the summer of 1988, it appeared that Soviet influence in the ANC was increasing significantly, largely because of the emergence of talented young SACP members.[48] The NEC was expanded to 35, and 3 of the 7 new members were also SACP members. Most observers consider Thabo Mbeki, a moderate SACP member, to be the likely successor of the aging Tambo. However, the militant chief of staff, Chris Hani, figures as an alternative in some estimates.

Whatever the outcome of this succession struggle between the ANC's militant and moderate wings, Moscow's chief instrument, the SACP, is getting stronger. Its membership increased 90 percent from the sixth congress in 1984 to the seventh in 1989, and it increasingly recruits inside South Africa on its own account, especially in the unions. The SACP's main objective is expanding its power in the unions, thus adding to its old power base in *Umkhonto*. Although successful to a considerable extent, SACP influence is somewhat retarded by militant union leaders who oppose the SACP's gradualist approach to revolution and socialism. SACP member Mac Maharaj coordinates the ANC organization in South Africa and is reportedly quite talented. Rising new stars like Alex Mushini and Mzala have begun to play a role in formulating and implementing policy. Even the constitutional guidelines for a future government were drafted under the chairmanship of a veteran Communist. Dr. Simon Makana, a member of the SACP Central Committee, heads the new ANC mission in Moscow, which virtually enjoys embassy status. In March 1989 Tambo met candidate Politburo member Anatoly Lukyanov, a close associate of Gorbachev and soon to be promoted to vice-president of the USSR. Tambo stressed that there was "no change whatsoever" in Moscow's support for the ANC.[49] Of course, Tambo is the first ANC head to meet with a CPSU general secretary (Gorbachev). It would require a dramatic turn of events to reverse this slow, steady increase in Soviet influence in the ANC. As Richard Staar put it, "The ANC is *almost* openly dominated by the Moscow-line Communist Party of South Africa" [emphasis added].[50]

As the new decade began, the SACP was somewhat disquieted by the pace of *glasnost* and *perestroika,* as reflected both in Joe Slovo's jousting with reformist CPSU ideologues in the Soviet media, and in the convening of the Seventh Congress of the SACP in Havana (June 1989) rather than in Moscow. But the SACP also demonstrated its versatility in January 1990 when Joe Slovo hinted that a multiparty system might be acceptable in a post-apartheid South Africa. One day before, Thabo Mbeki had publicly reminded the world that Soviet help had been indispensable to the survival of the SACP. Of course, the dramatic release of non-communist Nelson Mandela may dilute SACP influence. In evaluating SACP prospects, it is important to remember that the ANC presidential staff had been almost a SACP preserve for some time, that the SACP had recruited the cream of the Soweto generation of refugees into SACP ranks, and it had virtually controlled the education of key cadres for over a decade.

3

THE AFRICAN NATIONAL CONGRESS

A Complex and Evolving Soviet Relationship

The relationship between the USSR and the ANC is considerably more complex than is generally recognized, which is why merely counting the Communists on the ANC's ruling organs is somewhat misleading and provides limited insight into a rather fluid and dynamic process.[1]

Moscow does provide much of the military and economic support for the ANC, but few of the ANC's leaders are completely reliable instruments of Soviet foreign policy. An intricate mix of military, economic, and ideological factors and, above all, personal connections provides the USSR with significant influence inside the ANC, but Moscow certainly does not control it. The Kremlin's influence is very much conditioned by the state of flux in South African society. Thus, although the influence of the Soviet Union in the ANC rests on a much wider base than its communist membership, the depth of this influence—that is, the USSR's ability to dictate basic policy—remains constrained by countervailing cultural, political, and historical factors.

The Anti-Apartheid Act of 1986 directed the president of the United States to inform Congress "on the extent to which communists have infiltrated" organizations like the ANC,[2] although the SACP and the ANC have been openly and publicly allied since the early 1960s. The salient question is not who is, or who is not, a Communist, but what is the nature and extent of Soviet influence over the ANC, certainly one of the most significant political forces affecting South African society?

Although Soviet policy toward South Africa has been complex, inconsistent, and even contradictory at times, the major thrust seems to be to keep the pot simmering rather than boiling. The power of the South African security apparatus ensures that the ANC cannot seize power in the foreseeable future, and protracted repression gradually strengthens those inside the ANC most prone to violence and most dependent on Moscow for military aid. On the other hand, negotiations would provide a climate conducive to further diluting Soviet influence because bargaining, rather than violence, becomes the chief mode of gaining power. Thus the ANC's more pragmatic elements would be strengthened.

The pace and nature of change inside South Africa will probably condition the future relationship of the USSR and the ANC more than anything else. Whether the Soviet Union's influence inside the ANC increases or is diluted by the ANC's expanding relations with civic organizations and the burgeoning unions depends chiefly on initiatives in South Africa itself, not on external Soviet activities. Put another way, reform and negotiations among all the leaders of South African society are likely to retard Soviet influence whereas protracted violence is likely to enhance it because military aid is the major instrument of Soviet policy in the Third World.

Studies by some Soviet experts on South Africa betray an uneasiness about evolutionary change in the country, for dramatic progress toward the elimination of racial discrimination could severely attenuate, if not expunge, Soviet influence in the entire region.[3]

Ideological Diversity in the ANC

Ideologically, the ANC embraces a wide spectrum of opinions on such major issues as nationalization and the use of violence.[4] On the question of nationalization after seizing power, ANC opinion includes views ranging from support for complete government confiscation to forms of mixed economy, such as partial government ownership of stock in selected companies.[5]

It is doubtful that the ANC includes many people who "under normal circumstances fit quite comfortably into the Republican party," as one ANC official claimed; however, its guiding documents remain basically compatible with some form of welfare capitalism.[6] Of course, communist parties have a long history of publishing moderate programs while consolidating power.

In March 1988 a Swedish-funded project directed by ANC moderates adopted proposals that were far from a socialist commitment to nationalize the commanding heights of the economy; but the radicals, led by Chris Hani, opposed them.[7]

There is some confusion over the ideological commitments of young ANC recruits. One report suggests that youths arriving at the training camps ask to join the SACP, not the ANC.[8] But more recent reports claim that ANC recruits since 1976 have tended to be more nationalist than Marxist.[9] This confusion probably reflects the superficiality of the ideological outlook of the youths. As one black reporter in Soweto put it, "I'm not sure if everybody [ANC recruits] has a knowledge of what communism is, but as a show of defiance to the government, it [SACP membership] has a lot of appeal."[10] Former South African president P. W. Botha also thinks that most youths are not Communists.[11]

What is certain is that the youths are more radical on issues like nationalization and the use of violence, which does not mean they are communist or pro-Soviet. It is highly unlikely that they would want to substitute one master for another. In fact, before the ANC's Second Consultative Conference, held in 1985, reports indicated that younger ANC militants were restive about SACP influence, especially its restraint on random violence.[12]

The SACP's reluctance to support a policy of indiscriminate terrorism is nothing new and reflects Lenin's cautious attitude toward revolutionary violence. As one South African dissident, Richard Gibson, put it: "The communists continued to argue among themselves concerning the necessity of armed struggle later than most of their African proteges." As editor of the English-language edition of an African revolutionary journal, *Revolution*, Gibson had first-hand experience of that debate in London in 1963 and 1964.[13]

It is often forgotten that Marxism-Leninism emerged in the late nineteenth century as a rival to revolutionary terrorist movements in Russia. Lenin himself argued that random violence without cumulative effect is counterproductive. He called it the "sin of spontaneity" and "adventurism" because it produces a reaction before a strong organization and carefully orchestrated strategy could produce a successful revolution.[14]

A rigidly orthodox, intellectual party like the SACP is keenly aware of these Leninist injunctions. As Joe Slovo, the SACP secretary general (then chairman), put it in the summer of 1985: "No romantic illusions must be held about the speed with which apartheid can be destroyed." Slovo went on to argue that the upsurge in protest was spontaneous and semispontaneous and that the ANC's highest priority was to expand its underground cells.[15] This conforms to Lenin's prescription in his classic *State and Revolution*, where he calls for "arming the whole people" and putting the party in tune with the "spontaneous" masses before actually attempting to seize power.[16]

Attitudes of ANC Leadership Toward Violence

Although all the ANC's leaders support a policy of armed struggle, the difference of opinion between the ANC radicals and the veteran Communists (who are more conservative) is only one among several divisions of opinion within the ANC on the question of the appropriate strategy for using violence to achieve political ends. In the past, Nelson Mandela, the imprisoned ANC leader, has rejected any policy aimed at civilians.[17] Oliver Tambo, the ANC president, has opposed destruction of the economic infrastructure needed to run the country after seizing power.[18] Joe Slovo has advocated hitting what one might call soft military targets such as farms connected with military communication centers or shopping centers where police or military installations are located.[19] Some young radicals support a soft-target policy—striking purely civilian facilities, the quintessential terrorist strategy designed to render the society ungovernable and theoretically amenable to a transfer of power.[20]

At its secret Second Consultative Conference in Kabwe, north of the Zambian capital, Lusaka, between June 16 and 23, 1985, the ANC reached a compromise that rejected indiscriminate terrorism, which had never been its policy, but authorized its military wing to proceed with bombings with less concern for civilian casualties and without consulting the ruling NEC. This compromise makes it easier to deny responsibility when politically expedient.[21] In confirming that military installations will continue to be the prime targets, Tambo acknowledged that "in attacking military targets, all sorts of people will be hit. It is quite unavoidable."[22] But he reportedly condemned the May 1983 car bombing in Pretoria that resulted in 70 casualties—the bomb was next to a bus stop near air force headquarters and timed to go off at rush hour—as unforgivable negligence.[23]

For concrete reasons it is unlikely that any top ANC leader supports the killing of alleged collaborators by placing flaming tires around their necks (referred to as *necklacing*). First, it alienates influential people around the world who might be sympathetic to the ANC.[24] Second, from a communist viewpoint, necklacing is exactly the kind of random violence without cumulative effect that Lenin found counterproductive. Such horrifying practices certainly retard the prospects for either a revolution or a negotiated settlement by alienating support for the insurgents and intensifying repression. Some necklacing apparently involves merely private quarrels, provoking bitter reprisals and accelerating intra-African dissensions. Most necklacing is probably the work of young militants whom the ANC cannot control, although some ANC radicals apparently do support necklacing, suggesting the presence of severe extremists in the ranks.[25] This brutal and violent Fanonist element represents a wild card for the Soviets.

Tambo has discouraged necklacing: one report indicated that he sent a message to ANC militants telling them to stop the necklacing, adding that "my people should take this as a strong 'hint.'"[26] This is further evidence of the ANC's inability to control all its own cadres, much less militant nonmembers.

Whether the USSR and its clients are developing a policy more accommodating to terrorism remains to be seen. Certainly the continuing activities of the ANC-SACP alliance bear watching as events unfold in southern Africa. In this regard, it is worth noting that Nelson Mandela offered to help ameliorate the violence in a May 1986 meeting with members of the Eminent Persons Group, a Commonwealth investigating commission. But in July 1988 the ANC set off a huge bomb near a rugby sports stadium, with no military or economic targets even remotely nearby. The sophistication of this device suggests that orders came from headquarters. There were reportedly 25 somewhat similar bombing incidents by mid-1988.[27] This indicates an increasing tolerance for the deliberate killing of innocent citizens, the essence of terrorism.

The creation of a second layer of the ANC command structure, called Regional Political-Military Councils (RPMC), in the adjacent states designed to extend control down to the township street committees makes unauthorized bombings of the magnitude and sophistication of the rugby variety unlikely, although there is some evidence that these "'comrades' committees" are breaking down under pressure from the security apparatus.[28]

Internal Conflict: ANC vs. SACP

Although the ANC and SACP have been formally allied for years—an alliance confirmed at the 1985 Consultative Conference—there has been continuing friction between the two.[29] Generally speaking, ANC suspicion of the SACP emanates from three sources: fear of communist domination, resentment over the prominence of whites in the SACP, and concern that the

SACP, despite recent rhetoric, shares Moscow's present aversion to revolution.

A group of Marxist intellectuals were expelled from the ANC in the late 1970s because they considered the ANC's pro-Soviet members too moderate.[30] The suspicion remains among many Marxists in the ANC and close to it that the USSR is primarily interested in the propaganda value of the South African crisis, in maintaining a simmering pot, and that it does not want either a revolution or a transfer of power through negotiation and selective violence. These Marxists think Moscow's main concern is defaming and slandering the United States throughout the world as a racist and imperialist ally of South Africa. Highlighting the alleged Pretoria-Washington axis, of course, has been a continuous theme of Soviet public diplomacy. But some Marxists in the ANC see the SACP as a mere instrument of Soviet foreign policy and a vehicle for the purely Soviet objective of tarnishing the image of the United States.[31]

In an assessment of Soviet influence over the ANC, one must recognize that not only young ANC radicals but also many ANC Marxists are critical of the SACP as well as its Soviet patron. Inside the ANC, then, the SACP has its critics on the right and the left, as well as among the young, whereas the veterans in the SACP leadership increasingly seem to believe that the kind of bloodbath likely in a revolution would favor the Marxists, whom they designate by the communist epithet "Trotskyites."

Let us turn now to another long-standing source of concern and suspicion within the ANC—the white Communists. In 1975 some disenchanted ANC veterans (the Makiwane faction) bolted from the ranks in protest against excessive white communist influence,[32] which may have been why Joe Slovo, who is white, resigned as *Umkhonto* chief of staff in 1987 and was allegedly demoted from chairman to secretary general of the SACP. His replacement, Dan Tloome, is black. But as mentioned previously, the post of secretary general is too important in most communist parties to be regarded as a demotion.

To retard communist influence, the ANC president in 1973 encouraged the formation of a white-consciousness movement called *Okhela*,[33] and dissident ANC members organized the breakaway Pan-African Congress in 1959 to offset the excessive influence of white Communists.[34] Beginning in the 1940s, when both Nelson Mandela and Oliver Tambo called for the expulsion of Communists, who were then disproportionately white, ANC nationalists have been accusing Communists of attempting to seize control.[35] Thus friction between the ANC leadership and its communist members has a long history, although its implications should not be overstated, especially if conditions of severe and escalating violence and repression were to become the norm.

Friction Between the USSR and the ANC-SACP

The extent of Soviet influence over the ANC-SACP alliance has been somewhat exaggerated, largely because of the tendency to identify ANC members who are also SACP members as Soviet puppets who are virtual instruments of Soviet foreign policy. Although the SACP has adhered to Moscow's ideological line as strictly as any communist party outside the Soviet bloc, both it and the ANC have reason to be suspicious of the Kremlin. Also, with the coming of *glasnost'*, ideology is increasingly a source of friction.

The USSR has a long record of sacrificing local Communists to the interests of the Soviet state, the classic example being the Egyptian Communists who languished in jail while the relationship of Nasser and the Soviets prospered. More recently, the Soviets have sacrificed the interests of Iranian Communists to the USSR's national interest. In the late 1980s, some Soviet Africanists were suggesting that a consociation might be an acceptable solution to South Africa's crisis, contrary to the long-standing ANC-SACP insistence on a unitary state. In addition, Moscow maintains long-standing economic relationships with large South African commercial enterprises, which must be a significant source of suspicion for the ANC, a relatively ideologically rigid organization, although the more sophisticated members recognize the common interest of the USSR and South Africa in maintaining high prices for gold and strategic minerals.[36] In fact, a successful ANC revolt might lead to higher prices.

Another source of suspicion is the increasing Soviet contacts with black organizations other than the ANC.[37] These contacts include the ANC's most important rivals, such as the PAC and Zulu chief Gatsha Buthelezi, whose invitation to talk with Soviet diplomats in the United States in October 1982 was cordially accepted and widely known.[38]

Another serious potential source of tension between the ANC and Moscow is the question of ANC relations with China. A key condition for past Soviet aid was that the ANC support Moscow, not Beijing,[39] and by 1969 the USSR had virtually expunged Chinese influence from the ANC.[40] But in June 1983 Tambo paid a successful visit to Beijing, after a Chinese proclamation that conformed to the ANC policy line.[41] This followed a 1982 visit to ANC headquarters in Zambia by the Chinese prime minister. Despite this flurry of activity, the extent that such contacts antagonize the USSR should not be overstated. Moscow has been steadily improving its relations with China, and pragmatists in the Soviet decision-making apparatus may view Chinese activities as driving a wedge between Washington and Beijing—always a major Soviet foreign policy objective—because the effect of Chinese initiatives is to encourage armed struggle and retard U.S. efforts to facilitate an internal accommodation.

ANC Leaders Closely Associated with the USSR

As discussed previously, the youths who show up at ANC camps asking to join the SACP can hardly be labeled stooges of the Kremlin. Their prime motivation is undoubtedly exasperation at the pace of change as well as a simplistic anti-capitalism, rather than a sophisticated ideological commitment, much less loyalty to the USSR. Closest to Moscow are a few veteran SACP leaders and several middle-aged ANC personalities.

These ANC leaders can be designated as Soviet associated. Not all are known Communists, but even the non-Communists have had extended working relationships with the Soviet bloc. The term *pro-Soviet* is too strong because it indicates an automaton or puppetlike relationship, which is uncharacteristic of African intellectuals and charismatic personalities, which most of these leaders are. Even Soviet oriented or Soviet inclined is misleading because it suggests a unidirectional facing East and a Soviet predominance over the mind and actions of these important ANC figures. Soviet influenced is perhaps a more accurate description, but close personal relations—with the more moderate President Tambo, for example—or respect for Nelson Mandela may serve to counteract and attenuate Soviet influence in some cases, which helps explain why some accounts refer to pragmatic Communists. Also, for some individual Communists the ideals of African nationalism compete with the ideological tenets of Marxism-Leninism for these individuals' allegiance. Most ANC leaders are nationalists, as were Tito and Mao, who, though communist, were certainly not Soviet puppets. When you are evaluating Soviet influence in the Third World, remember that Communists are usually nationalists and often anti-Soviet.

Nevertheless, some important ANC figures have associated extensively with the Soviet bloc and with Communists more than other ANC figures and are thus the most likely to serve as conduits for Soviet efforts to influence the ANC. These associations and working relationships are briefly outlined below.[42]

All the ANC figures discussed here are members of the ANC's ruling NEC. To begin with, neither the ANC's leader, Nelson Mandela, nor its president, Oliver Tambo, nor its secretary general, Alfred Nzo, nor its military commander, Joe Modise, are Communists. Nzo did receive the order of Lenin, and Tambo received the Star of International Friendship Order in Gold from East Germany, but this hardly makes either a Soviet puppet. Tambo is a Western-trained lawyer, and no one considers him a Communist. However, his moderation is sometimes exaggerated because his published statements have tended to follow the Soviet line, even on non-African subjects. Nzo emphatically denies that he is a Communist, but he certainly has strong Soviet connections. For instance, he is a vice-president of the World Peace Council, a recognized Soviet-front organization.[43] Thomas Nkobi, ANC treasurer, although he may not formally be an SACP member, is probably close to the Soviets because most ANC funds have come from Moscow in the past. However, only about half may now originate in the Soviet bloc. In any case, none of these top ANC leaders are clearly pro-Soviet, much less controlled by the Kremlin. However, confidential interviews with ANC connections by the author confirm that even the most moderate ANC leaders maintain channels of communication with the Soviets that are completely separate and distinct from those of the SACP.

Among the veteran SACP leaders on the NEC, four figures appear to be the keys to Moscow's influence in the ANC. Mzwai Pilaso has headed intelligence and personnel since 1981 and must work closely with the extensive KGB network in southern Africa. Pilaso works closely with the more moderate President Tambo and is often listed as his special aide. Dan Tloome is the new SACP chairman, based in Lusaka, Zambia. He served as chief of undercover operations for sixteen years (1964–1980) in Botswana, a major *Umkhonto* infiltration route. Joe Slovo has been discussed above. Stephen Dlamini heads the South African Congress of Trade Unions, the banned ANC union, and is a veteran SACP member.

Another important SACP figure is Mac Maharaj, the top Indian, who is part of a younger group (still relatively middle-aged) of SACP leaders that includes Chris Hani, *Umkhonto* chief of staff. Both Maharaj and Hani are on the SACP Politburo along with Steve Tswete. Also included in this younger group are figures who are probably not formal SACP members but who have career patterns reflecting extensive Soviet connections. For instance, Dr. Francis Meli, who received a doctorate at the University of Leipzig in East Germany, wrote his dissertation on the Comintern, the chief vehicle for Soviet control of the world communist movement in the 1920s and 1930s. He is editor of the pro-Soviet ANC journal *Sechaba*, which is edited in London but printed in East Germany. In 1986, Meli visited San Francisco at the invitation of the Communist Party, USA.[44] Sizakele Sigxashe was educated in the USSR and is chief ANC intelligence analyst. James Stuart seems to have been in contact with the Soviets while representing the ANC in Madagascar. Tony Mongale headed the ANC office in East Berlin.

Aziz Pahad, an expert on the South African military, and Ruth Mompati may be SACP members, but there is some evidence that they support more moderate, pragmatic policies. John Nkadimeng is on the SACP Politburo. Ronnie Kasrils, the second white on the NEC, is chief of ANC military intelligence and a member of the SACP Central Committee. Cassius Make, who was assassinated in 1987, had supervised the important Angolan training camps and other operations since 1976, but as a younger radical, he may have held this post precisely to restrain the Communists and constrain Soviet influence because some sources have reported a subtle effort to recruit non-Marxist radical nationalists since 1976.[45]

To recapitulate, it is indisputable that major figures in the ANC have had extensive contacts with the USSR over the years. Many nuances and mitigating circumstances, however, condition Soviet influence in this organization, which is clearly in a state of flux within a sea of societal change. A handful of prominent ANC personages seem to be virtual instruments of Soviet foreign policy; others are more pragmatic Communists. Some are not Communists at all, but have long career patterns reflecting extensive communist contacts. Some non-Communists have separate channels of communication with the USSR because they are leaders. But most of the top figures are not Communists and have lived through a long history of resisting excessive communist influence.

Many experienced the nonviolent pre-1960 period of ANC history, and some are known to have religious convictions. Albert Luthuli, the ANC's president in the 1950s, was a Methodist lay preacher whose principled belief in nonviolent protest earned him the Nobel Peace Prize. Like many early black protest leaders, he possessed an optimism inspired by black Americans like Booker T. Washington and early Christian mission teachers. Today President Oliver Tambo is a Christian, and there is an official ANC chaplain (Rev. Fumanelike Gquiba), but there is no evidence of widespread Christian services in the ANC camps. Christian ideals like African nationalism, however, may still compete with Marxism-Leninism for the hearts and minds of the young, as well as the NEC's old guard; a major ANC ally inside South Africa is the UDF, which is heavily influenced by church leaders.[46]

Conclusion

The future relationship of the USSR to the ANC may gradually be conditioned by the rise to the leadership of large numbers of youths educated in the Soviet Union. Of the fifteen hundred ANC students who have scholarships to study abroad, approximately four hundred study in the Soviet bloc.[47] Such study, however, is no guarantee of future affinity, especially since racist attitudes toward Africans are widespread on the Soviet streets and to a lesser extent in the universities.

Although Soviet influence in the ANC is substantial, there are many reasons to conclude that the Soviet Union will not totally control the ANC in the short run. First, there are specific reasons why the ANC harbors deep suspicions of Soviet motives and vice versa. Second, the USSR has always found that manipulating charismatic personalities and intellectuals in Africa is no easy task, as their experiences with the first presidents of Marxist Angola and Mozambique illustrate. Third, the USSR has a certain disdain for the ANC, which will probably limit Soviet commitments. Fourth is the USSR's proven willingness to sacrifice vital ANC interests for short-term Soviet gains, such as acquiescing in the removal of ANC bases from Mozambique in 1984. Fifth, prominent Soviet figures have called for retaining some racial classifications in a post-apartheid constitution. Sixth, Soviet acceptance of the ANC's expulsion from all its Angolan military bases in 1989 infuriates the young cadres. As one SACP spokesman put it, "Asoyan [second deputy chief of the African Department of the Soviet Foreign Ministry] seems to reduce the liberation struggle to some nuisance factor in the international fight for peace. This is unacceptable as our war of liberation is a part of the struggle for world peace." [48] Finally, the interlocking and overlapping relationships with civic organizations and unions may dilute, rather than enhance, Soviet influence, especially in a context of reform and negotiation.

In the late 1980s, official Soviet rhetoric called for a political settlement that would end apartheid, provoking some analysts to predict a change in Moscow's basic strategy. Of course, the Kremlin would prefer a settlement that would enhance its national interests and that of its clients as much as possible, and it probably will employ its new contacts with the South Africans and its African diplomatic initiatives with the Western nations toward this end. Certainly Soviet initiatives to develop a joint approach with the Americans to the South African question represent an effort to pressure the regime to deal with the ANC. Unlike the costly and expensive Angolan counterinsurgency, however, denouncing apartheid and supporting the modest armed struggle are relatively cheap, and historically these have proved to be a most cost-effective means of enhancing Soviet influence and prestige, especially in the Third World. Shortly after ANC president Oliver Tambo's 1989 visit to Moscow, the USSR confirmed its commitment to armed struggle. Soviet first deputy foreign affairs minister Anatoly Adamishin threatened, "Those who think we are going to stop supplying the ANC with arms to force it into negotiations are engaging in wishful thinking." Adamishin went on to hint that the USSR might be interested in playing a mediating role, if the government and the ANC decided to negotiate, to avoid being shut out of a settlement, as it was in Zimbabwe in 1979. The Soviets would like to get some credit for facilitating an accommodation both as a face-saving measure and as the best means of preserving some residual influence. In the 1988 Angola-Namibia negotiations, the USSR was only moderately successful with a similar approach.[49]

In short, the decisive factor conditioning both Soviet involvement and Soviet influence is the perceived prospect of genuine reform and negotiations among representatives of all the leading political forces of South African society. An accommodation would remove the chronic instability that has been the foundation of Soviet influence in the region.

4

NAMIBIA

The USSR and SWAPO

Since 1963 the centerpiece and chief instrument of Soviet policy for Namibia has been the insurgent SWAPO. Namibia's increasing importance for Soviet policy was underlined in 1984 when a report in *Pravda* indicated that this obscure, faraway state was discussed at Politburo meetings.[1] One Soviet analyst even concluded that Namibia was Moscow's most important concern in southern Africa,[2] and one of the first acts of Gorbachev's foreign minister, Shevardnadze, was a highly publicized meeting with SWAPO leader Sam Nujoma in Algeria.[3] Six months later the SWAPO leader spent two very visible weeks in Moscow. *Pravda* published an interview in which Nujoma declared "the only way out is to seek independence by force of arms."[4]

In 1988, SWAPO opened a mission in Moscow. Unlike the ANC, SWAPO was recognized by the U.N. and the OAU as the authentic representative of the Namibian people, but not as the government. Since 1966 SWAPO had sponsored an extended insurgency against various administrations supported by South Africa. The following analysis focuses first on the escalating Cuban involvement with SWAPO in 1988 and then on the complex, evolving relationship of SWAPO with the USSR.

Joint SWAPO–Cuban Operations in 1988

South African security forces had nearly decimated SWAPO by raids into SWAPO sanctuaries in southern Angola from 1978 to 1988, even though these bases are often guarded by Cuban and Angolan troops and ringed with Soviet radar and tanks. In the spring of 1988, however, Cuba suddenly inserted at least 10,000 crack new troops through the port of Namibe into Angola's fifth military district, along the Namibian border, where SWAPO sanctuaries are located,[5] bringing the Cuban total in Angola to approximately 50,000.[6]

Until 1988 Cuban troops generally fought alongside SWAPO in SWAPO sanctuaries, after SWAPO had retreated into a fortified position; but in June of that year Cuban troops maneuvered in joint combat units with SWAPO close to the Namibian border, implicitly threatening for the first time to attack. In a front-page article on May 2, 1988, the official Cuban daily, *Granma*, lauded the "audacious and unstoppable movements of Cuban/Angolan/SWAPO forces."[7]

When South Africa warned against an attack on Namibia, Fidel Castro retorted that Pretoria was "in no position to demand anything."[8] Furthermore, a Cuban official stated that "we are not saying that we will not go into Namibia."[9] These actions seemed to reinforce Castro's warning in 1987 that Cuba would remain in southern Africa until apartheid fell.[10]

This effectively resuscitated SWAPO's sagging fortunes. At the very least, the presence of fresh Cuban troops with SWAPO served to slow, if not curtail completely, South African military initiatives not only in Angola but also in Namibia. The joint maneuvers took place at the end of the rainy season, when SWAPO usually sends small guerrilla units into Namibia. In effect, Cuban behavior suggested that it was moving from a passive-defensive role to an offensive one, escalating the military stakes to bring South Africa to accept a negotiated settlement in both Angola and Namibia. As Castro put it in a meeting with African diplomats, Cuba "is in a position to take more military risks, for if the enemy wants a confrontation, he can suffer a serious defeat."[11] Because it focused specifically on the fifth military district, this Cuban operation was calculated to affect the Namibian situation. The operation's magnitude and timing are worth noting in some detail.

The fifth military region, adjacent to Namibia and the major SWAPO infiltration route from Angola into Namibia, is served by the port of Namibe, a major Soviet facility for supplying SWAPO and the combined Angolan, Cuban, and ANC units that operate against the Angolan rebels, UNITA.

In November 1987 the fifth military region had one Cuban anti-aircraft brigade and one Cuban mechanized regiment. In December more-experienced Cuban officers began to appear in Angola, and by March 11 a massive movement of Cuban troops into southern Angola had commenced.[12] By June 1988 the addition of up to ten thousand Cuban troops increased the overall Cuban presence by about 25 percent, and the situation changed dramatically.

A new strategic headquarters was established at Lubango with General Ochoa Sanchez in overall command. A member of the Cuban Communist Party's Central Committee, he had combat command experience in Angola, Ethiopia, and Nicaragua.

The new troops included Cuba's best pilots and an armored division that had up to four hundred T-55 and T-62 tanks; six rifle regiments with fifteen and twenty thousand men each; one artillery regiment with 122-mm D-30 guns, 122-mm BM-21 and 240-mm BM-24 multiple rocket launchers; and an air defense regiment with SA-2, SA-3, SA-6, SA-8, and SA-13 surface-to-air missiles; and two SU-23–4 anti-aircraft systems supported by an array of radar support, including Flatface, Spoonrest, and Barlock systems.[13]

The Cuban contingents were supported by three joint Cuban-SWAPO battalions, each comprised of approximately 200 Cuban and 250 SWAPO personnel. Each battalion had a joint Cuban-SWAPO command, as well as armor and artillery support.[14]

The airfield at Xangongo, 37 miles from Namibia, was enlarged to provide additional support capability, and the joint Cuban-SWAPO Tiger battalion was stationed there. This base was extremely well protected by Soviet air defense systems; thus it was the key SWAPO sanctuary. Slightly further north were the other joint battalions, Zebra at Mupa and Lion at Cahama.[15] The positioning suggested preparations for supporting the most dramatic incursion into Namibia by SWAPO yet, either by direct support or more likely by diverting the attention of the South African forces while the guerrillas infiltrate.

The Battle of Calueque Dam: June 1988

In June 1988, despite Cuban participation in ongoing negotiations for a settlement, it was reported that Castro personally ordered his crack 50th Division to advance to the Namibian border to confront South African forces dug in around the Calueque Dam, which supplies water and electricity to northern Namibia.[16] Often described as Castro's personal division, the 50th is rated as one of the best fighting units in the regular Cuban army and has been used to guard the U.S. base at Guantanamo in Cuba.

In early June 1988 a combined Angolan-Cuban-SWAPO force with the 50th Division at its core advanced to Xangongo and then to Ngiva, about seventeen miles from the Namibian border. On June 27 a joint force of six hundred infantry and 35 tanks attacked the Calueque Dam immediately north of the Namibian border (approximately nine miles). Cuban aircraft reportedly bombed the dam even though Cuban envoys at a conference in Brazzaville, Congo, had promised not to do so.

Although the fighting ended in a stalemate, with substantial casualties on both sides, the Cubans demonstrated an aggressiveness that threatened Namibia itself. SWAPO was much better positioned for guerrilla operations. The Cuban and Angolan pilots flew reconnaissance missions over northern Namibia, where key South African bases were located. They also flew dash sorties, apparently to provoke air combat, and there were some skirmishes along the border.[17] When South Africa bombarded Cuban positions on July 26 at Techipa, MIG-23s responded by again raiding Calueque, damaging the Calueque bridge, which restricted South Africa's options and disrupted the water supply to Owambo in Namibia. A motorized rifle regiment also counterattacked, killing eleven South Africans. There is also some evidence that Soviet Frog surface-to-surface missiles, capable of hitting South African bases, had been deployed.[18]

Although an invasion of Namibia was unlikely, these missiles and the air power might have facilitated SWAPO incursions, for this Cuban initiative represented a major escalation that strengthened and encouraged SWAPO. It also bolstered the Cuban position in any negotiations for a settlement.

July saw the installation of 150 SAM-8 missile batteries, the most advanced in the Soviet arsenal, linked to sophisticated radar systems designed to monitor South African air bases along the Namibian border. Work was also completed on two key air bases at Xangongo and Cahama in southern Angola. Not just airstrips, these bases included hangars, maintenance facilities, and supply dumps, which permitted their operation as forward bases threatening Namibia. In short, Cuban and Soviet military prestige had been committed to mitigate the air power so vital to South Africa's military superiority in southern Angola and northern Namibia.

In September five thousand more troops reportedly left Cuba, setting the stage for a major engagement if the ongoing peace talks broke down. On November 1 the Namibian independence process did not begin as planned, and rumors in Namibia suggested that South Africa was not preparing to withdraw for at least two years. The South Africans claimed that, in violation of an August agreement, Cuba had moved its entire 50th Division south near the Namibian border. In mid-November, however, Cuban and South African negotiators tentatively reached a preliminary agreement to withdraw from Angola and Namibia, respectively, over a 27-month period, and in December a final accord was signed.

The Bush War in Northern Namibia and Southern Angola: 1966–1988

The history of the bush war between SWAPO and South Africa is one of gradual escalation of Soviet involvement over more than two decades. Although SWAPO received some arms and training from the USSR before 1969, it was not until then that Moscow confirmed SWAPO as the legitimate "liberation" movement for Namibia.[19] U.N. recognition did not come until 1973. The Kremlin and its surrogates then expanded the training of SWAPO at facilities in the USSR, Eastern Europe, Cuba, and ultimately Angola.[20] Trainees frequently arrive from East Germany in particular.[21]

In the latter half of the 1970s, military assistance included large quantities of small arms, rocket launchers, personnel carriers, the protection of Soviet tanks, and sophisticated air defense systems, as well as Cuban, East German, and Angolan troops inside Angola.

By 1987 Lubango airport in southern Angola, the chief airbase protecting and supporting SWAPO, hosted a squadron of MIG-23 fighters, MI-24 helicopters, and various Soviet-made anti-aircraft radar units manned by Soviets and East Europeans. A Cuban unit protected these facilities.[22] In 1985 estimates of SWAPO's military strength ranged from 6,400 to 8,500, although one specialist suggested that "fewer than 20 percent were operational at one time." Approximately 10,000 SWAPO soldiers were available in 1988.[23]

From the insurgency's beginning in August 1966 until 1984, SWAPO suffered an estimated 8,200 killed.[24] The bush war between SWAPO and the South African administration intensified in the early 1980s. South African forces reportedly killed approximately one thousand SWAPO soldiers and two Russian colonels in Operation Protea inside Angola in July 1981. A Russian sergeant major was captured along with roughly $200 million worth of equipment, mostly of communist origin.[25] In Operation Super, March 1982, near SWAPO headquarters at Mupa in southern Angola, some 201 SWAPO troops were killed.[26]

SWAPO claims to have initiated 802 armed actions from November 1981 to November 1982.[27] Having infiltrated white farms in northern Namibia in April and May 1982, SWAPO launched a series of incursions in January 1983 into Ovamboland and Kavango. Approximately 203 were killed in the latter incursion and as many as 918 in all of 1983. Despite these devastating losses, however, one specialist argues that SWAPO increased its influence in the Kavango province of northern Namibia.[28] Some confirmation of this can be found in the designation of Kavango and other provinces bordering Angola as security areas in March 1985.[29] Nevertheless, SWAPO influence is strongest among the Ovambo people.

In Operation Askari, which took place from December 3, 1983, until February 1, 1984, an estimated four hundred SWAPO, Angolan, and Cuban troops were killed. Twenty-five tanks were destroyed along with tons of equipment, including sophisticated air defense systems made by the Soviets and installed by East Germans.[30]

In summary, by 1988 SWAPO had made little military progress against the powerful and aggressive South African Defense Force (SADF), even though SWAPO was supported inside Angola by Cuban, East German, and Angolan forces. Nevertheless, there was some evidence that SWAPO's political influence was growing in Namibia. Evidence that SWAPO fought well during Operation Askari in the heavy fighting at Ongiva, Cahama, and Cuvelai[31] suggested a better quality of training and trainees.

The commitment of Cuban troops to combat in Operation Askari was also something new, which encouraged SWAPO. After fighting in the front lines during the initial intervention in Angola in 1975–1976, the Cubans appeared reluctant to engage in combat. Their morale was low and they were considered unreliable,[32] which was a far cry from 1976, when veteran reporter Ian Smiley found himself "retreating in front of an oncoming wave of Cuban tanks."[33]

In early 1983 Castro specifically instructed his troops not to engage the South Africans.[34] By the mid-1980s, however, the commitment of Cuban pilots to help protect SWAPO sanctuaries and the more frequent meetings with high Soviet officials dramatically improved SWAPO morale. In early 1988 SWAPO proudly claimed to have shot down two South African planes with its own missiles.[35]

Although SWAPO suffered enormous casualties proportionately, this is not unusual in guerrilla warfare and may enhance its prestige inside Namibia and with the USSR. Because SWAPO depends on the Soviet Union and its surrogates for arms and military training, Moscow's grip may tighten.

Soviet Influence Over SWAPO

The relationship between SWAPO and the USSR is more complex than is generally recognized. Until recently, 90 percent of SWAPO military equipment came from the USSR. As the Kremlin recognizes, however, there are many factions within SWAPO,[36] most of whom are probably genuine nationalists, as identified initially by the totally Soviet-dominated SACP.[37]

Even though Sam Nujoma, the SWAPO president, was permitted by Soviet officials to publish in the Soviet party's theoretical journal, his organization is called a national-patriotic movement, not a vanguard party like that of Ethiopia.[38] Herman Toivo Ja Toivo, released from prison and elected

SWAPO's secretary general in 1985, has impeccable nationalist credentials.[39]

Soviet influence is greatest among those whom Moscow trains and arms, in this case SWAPO's military wing, which is apparently a semiautonomous body.[40] In the past, the USSR has expressed its unhappiness over SWAPO cadres' poor military performance, so there has been friction between the military wing and the Kremlin as well as between the more nationalist politicians in SWAPO, despite Moscow's role as chief armorer. Ever since the USSR abstained from the U.N. resolution calling for Namibian independence,[41] SWAPO suspicion of Soviet motives has been high.

The ambivalence of Soviet ideologues toward SWAPO relates to its external relations as well as to its internal organization and intentions. Talk of a Zimbabwe-like regime in Namibia by high-ranking SWAPO officials like Moses Garoeb irritates the Soviets. In November 1981 Garoeb, then secretary general, proclaimed that SWAPO would pursue the Zimbabwe model and specifically called for a pragmatic economic policy and a prohibition against the use of Namibia for attacks on South Africa by ANC guerrillas.[42] Both policies would represent setbacks for Moscow, which prefers a highly centralized command economy and tends to prefer instability and protracted conflict. The latter two increase the influence of its clients' military wings, which generally depend on Soviet arms and training.

The opening of a Moscow office in 1989 indicated growing Soviet confidence in SWAPO. Also, the close cooperation between Cuba and SWAPO enhanced Soviet influence with the insurgents. At the 1988 battle of Calueque Dam, the joint SWAPO-Cuban units fought and died together.[43] This offensive was very different from previous conflicts, where SWAPO fled into Cuban garrisons for protection. The virtual totalitarian nature of SWAPO also encourages Moscow: SWAPO has never held a congress and is the most rigidly centralized party in southern Africa.

By the summer of 1988 there was basically a military stalemate in the Namibia-Angola bush war that was costly for all concerned. The USSR and its auxiliaries had demonstrated the willingness and the ability to gradually escalate their military involvement to protect their client, SWAPO. Although support for the insurgency was Moscow's major policy instrument for Namibia, diplomatic and political efforts to establish a Soviet role at a very high level in the settlement process, as a joint guarantor of the peace with the United States, represented a complementary approach to increasing the Kremlin's influence while globally projecting an image of parity and equality with the other superpower.

In the December 1988 accords, the United States and the USSR emerged as observers, not guarantors, on the commission to monitor the withdrawal of South African and Cuban troops from Namibia and Angola, respectively.

In early 1989 high Soviet officials visited South Africa covertly and overtly at least four times in their observer capacity.[44] Moscow even attempted to appoint a KGB officer as an observer. In addition, the Kremlin began to transfer its intelligence presence from the capital of Angola to the capital of Namibia.[45] Moscow had achieved an internationally sanctioned presence in Namibia, one previously denied it. It had, however, been denied a military victory in Angola despite a massive effort for more than a decade, and South Africa continued to refuse Soviet requests for transferring the strategic naval base at Walvis Bay to Namibia.

5

ANGOLA

Three Decades of Intervention

Soviet intervention in Angola is an extended case study of how Moscow conducts its coercive diplomacy far from its periphery. The magnitude of communist involvement for a decade and a half constitutes an unparalleled projection of power into a distant area.

Although calling for political settlements of regional conflicts throughout the world, the new Gorbachev regime has pursued a significantly more assertive military strategy in Angola. In an August 1987 meeting with the new president of Mozambique, Gorbachev called for a "collective effort" to resolve the region's problems at the very moment that the USSR was encouraging and completely supplying a massive military offensive in the region.[1]

At the 27th Party Congress in February 1986, Gorbachev suggested that a political settlement to all regional conflicts was possible, but this was followed by no attenuation of Soviet activities in southern Africa. In fact, there was a significant escalation of Soviet military involvement in the region, particularly in Angola, where, despite rhetoric to the contrary, the USSR and especially its Cuban ally appeared to be seeking a confrontation.[2] These Soviet activities seem to be part of Moscow's new public diplomacy strategy, whereby more advantages are extracted from U.S. international political vulnerabilities by aggravating latent anti-Americanism.[3] What follows is a detailed analysis of Soviet coercive diplomacy in Angola.

An Evolving Strategy: From Garrison to Counterinsurgency to Quasi War

The Soviet Union and its allies have protected Angola's Marxist government since 1976, when they installed it in power. Although their forces were deployed with some restraint and caution, force levels were steadily increased, along with more sophisticated equipment and tactics.

The Friendship Treaty between the USSR and Angola does not automatically call for the Soviets to intervene, and Soviet behavior indicated that although it would defend Angola, the extent of its involvement would vary with the perceived threat. When the threat was from a low-level guerrilla insurgency in the early 1980s, Soviet activities could be characterized as a citadel strategy: the main towns were fortified, and the Angolan army would sally forth on occasion to keep the insurgents off balance.

As the insurgency became more successful and South African involvement grew, particularly after Operation Askari in 1983, Moscow and its allies seemed to adopt a new strategy designed to methodically destroy the insurgents in what amounted to a major escalation. By 1988 a further escalation revealed a new strategic emphasis that would confront the South African military and perhaps threaten Namibia. In June of that year the Cuban presence exceeded 45,000, up from about 37,000 the year before.[4] By October there were close to 60,000 (see table 4).

TABLE 4
SOVIET AND ALLIED FORCES IN ANGOLA 1987

Source of troops	Troops
USSR	2,500
East German	2,500
Cuban	37,000[a]
Angolan	80,000
SWAPO	7,000
ANC	1,200
Ex-Katangan	1,400

SOURCE: *Jane's Defense Weekly,* October 24, 1987, p. 950.

[a]According to Castro, by June 1988 there were over 45,000; by October close to 60,000, (*Jane's Defense Weekly,* August 19, 1989, p. 297).

TABLE 5
ESCALATING SOVIET MILITARY AID TO ANGOLA 1956–1987

	Level of aid
1956 to 1974	$63 million[a]
1977 to 1982	1 billion
1982 to 1984	2 billion
1986 to 1987	1 billion
1987 to 1988	1 billion

SOURCE: Michael H. Armacost, "Regional Issues and U.S.-Soviet Relations," U.S. Department of State, Current Policy No. 1089, June 22, 1988, p. 5.
[a]This figure is in millions, not billions, and includes nonmilitary aid. (Bruce D. Porter, *The USSR in Third World Conflicts* [Cambridge: Cambridge University Press, 1984], p. 156).

Since 1982 there has been a substantial escalation of Soviet involvement in Angola that amounted to a much more assertive strategy. Soviet involvement in Angola has steadily increased since 1956, when the Portuguese and Angolan communist parties helped form the MPLA, which in 1988 was the ruling Marxist government. The massive intervention on behalf of the MPLA at the time of independence from Portugal in 1975–1976 was followed by a lull and even a slight cutback in communist involvement, particularly of Cuban troops, until 1977, when a gradual step-up of support began (see table 5).[5] Over the next decade the USSR supplied about $4 billion worth of military equipment. Three-fourths of that $4 billion, however, arrived after 1982; from the summer of 1986 to the summer of 1987 an estimated $1 billion poured in. Another $1 billion arrived in 1987–1988.

Moscow's new assertiveness was reflected in two other developments. First, Cuban troops fought as combat units, not just as a garrison force in the major towns. Two thousand more Cuban troops arrived in 1986–1987 and more than ten thousand in 1988.[6] Second, Soviet advisers were attached to each battalion of the Angolan army when it went into combat, as distinguished from merely serving as technical advisers for the anti-aircraft defenses and as strategic planners. The Soviet troops helped operate the hardware.[7]

Early Soviet Involvement 1956–1975

Soviet interest in Angola extends back at least to the mid-1950s.[8] Soviet intelligence operatives are known to have been active in Angola since the early 1960s, and cadres of the MPLA were members of the Angolan Communist Party in 1956, when it was founded.[9] According to Bruce Porter, the U.S. State Department estimated Soviet aid to MPLA before 1974 at $63 million.[10] Another source calculates that Soviet arms shipments to the MPLA between 1960 and 1974 amounted to $67.5 million.[11]

In 1974 a military coup in Portugal, later supported by the Communists, set the stage for Angola's independence on November 11, 1975, but a civil war broke out in which the USSR and Cuba massively intervened to install the MPLA in power. The rival FNLA withered away, but another rival in the south, UNITA, led by Dr. Jonas Savimbi, continued to fight an increasingly successful guerrilla war.

Soviet activities before and during the civil war provide important insights into the Soviet foreign policy process. These activities reflect a certain ineptitude, vacillation, hesitation, and then an extraordinary decisiveness and creativity.

The ineptitude is most apparent immediately prior to the major intervention in 1975. Twice in the early 1970s, just before their historic intervention, the Soviets fell out with the leader of their client MPLA and shifted support from the highly intellectual poet-doctor Augustino Neto to the soldierly Daniel Chipenda, who ultimately fought with an invading South African force during the 1975–1976 civil war. In January 1973 Neto was reconciled with the USSR after a conference with Boris Ponomarev, the head of the International Department of the CPSU. But when the coup in Portugal occurred in April 1974, the Soviets again withheld assistance because of MPLA infighting and bickering. According to a high-level Soviet defector, Moscow did not trust Neto and considered him psychologically unreliable, but it ultimately supported him to please other African leaders.[12]

The Soviet-Cuban Intervention 1974–1976

In December 1974 the USSR sent 250 MPLA cadres to Moscow for military training. It had resumed arms shipments in August, and by January 1975 enough had arrived to equip a force of five thousand to seven thousand.[13] This set the stage for the U.S. government's decision that month to provide substantial covert aid to the rival FNLA, which had been receiving some aid since 1961.

Between February and April several large Soviet arms shipments for MPLA arrived in the Angolan capital, Luanda, along with two delegations from the Soviet Committee for Afro-Asian Solidarity, which often serves as a channel for arms to insurgents. One shipment had been flown from Brazzaville in the Congo in March.[14] With the Soviet arms flowing in, an agreement between the three insurgent movements (MPLA, FNLA, UNITA) to form a coalition government withered away and civil war loomed.

The Escalation: May 1975–February 1976

According to Cuban deputy premier Carlos Rafael Rodriguez, his government sent 230 military advisers to Angola in May 1975, before any U.S. arms had arrived.[15] In August MPLA asked the USSR for troops, but Russia declined and recommended Cuba, which sent two hundred more instructors but no troops. In early September Cuban military personnel left by ship for Angola, arriving on October 4, 7, and 11 to set up four training centers.[16] On November 5 the Cubans sent 650 elite security troops, and the next day a ship carrying an artillery regiment and a mechanized battalion left, arriving in Angola on November 27. From November 7 to December 9 at least 70 flights—carefully coordinated with the Soviets—supplied the Cuban expeditionary force. Although a U.S. diplomatic initiative halted the flights until December 24 after the U.S. Congress had cut off aid to the anti-MPLA forces, they then resumed on a massive scale, as seen in table 6.

There were between 170 and 400 Soviet advisers with the MPLA at the height of the war. Soviet IL-62 transport planes were ferrying aid from Cuba. The Soviets also deployed a small naval force that actually fired on the anti-MPLA forces and sent some MIGs that were never used. With the United States out of the conflict, these planes weren't necessary as the Soviet-backed Cubans and MPLA forces overran the country and Savimbi withdrew into the bush, from which he has gradually emerged.

The Soviets had been quick to take advantage of the power vacuum resulting from the cutoff of U.S. funding and support. Much has been made of the fact that Cuba apparently initiated the intervention. Given the long history of Soviet involvement and the fact that much of the logistical support and all of the financial support came from the USSR, perhaps this is overdone.

Moscow Confronts South Africa: 1983–1984

In November 1983 Soviet officials at the United Nations quietly, but dramatically, invoked something like the Brezhnev Doctrine in a warning to South Africa about the extent of its direct and indirect involvement in Angola.[17] The USSR had satellite reconnaissance photographs and other intel-

TABLE 6
ESCALATING CUBAN INVOLVEMENT IN ANGOLAN CIVIL WAR
OF 1975–1976

Date	Troops
November 15, 1975	2,000
November 20, 1975	3,000
November 30, 1975	3,000–5,000
December 20, 1975	4,000–6,000
January 6, 1976	9,500
February 3, 1976	12,000–14,000
Late April 1976	15,000

SOURCE: Bruce D. Porter, *The USSR in Third World Conflicts* (Cambridge: Cambridge University Press, 1984), p. 156.

ligence data about preparation for a major South African incursion into Angola (Operation Askari).[18]

Of equal concern to Moscow was the progress of the UNITA insurgency against Moscow's client, the ruling MPLA regime. UNITA controlled or was very active in ten of the nation's fourteen provinces and had infiltrated 90 miles northeast of Luanda, raising the prospect of defeat and overthrow of the MPLA. Although UNITA now enjoys increasing support from many sources, South African backing was essential in November 1983.

In an extraordinary private meeting at the Algonquin Hotel in New York, reportedly arranged by U.N. Secretary General Perez de Cuellar at Moscow's request, the USSR implicitly threatened South Africa but remained ambiguous about the specific action it would take if the MPLA's grip on Angola began to disintegrate completely from either South African or UNITA initiatives or both.

At the same time, in a direct show of force, the Kremlin dispatched the most powerful naval force since 1979 to round the Cape of Good Hope: an aircraft carrier and three surface vessels that stopped in the Angolan capital to underline the Kremlin's commitment to its client.

Soviet naval demonstrations are increasing with its naval power and serve as a signal of Moscow's determination to protect clients under the Brezhnev Doctrine. Soviet warships actually fired on opponents of its clients in both Angola (1975) and Ethiopia (1977). They threatened to do so in Mozambique (1981).

In December 1983 a substantial South African force (Operation Askari) attacked facilities of the Soviet-supported Namibian insurgent movement

(SWAPO) inside Angola and in the process encountered and defeated the Angolan army's 11th Brigade, which was guarding Cuvelai.

In reaction, the USSR delivered a public warning in early January 1984 through its Tass news agency that was similar to the private warning in November. Then the Kremlin convened a conference with Cuban and Angolan representatives to discuss the " defenses, independence, and territorial integrity" of Angola. At this point the South African advance halted.

Apparently the Soviet-Cuban-Angolan conference agreed to increase Soviet surrogate involvement, if not dramatically then at least significantly. Most important, the Angolans reportedly shed some of their reluctance to authorize Cubans and Soviets to pilot their combat aircraft.[19] This suggested that Cuban, Soviet, and perhaps even East German pilots might fly missions more frequently than the occasional mission of the past.

The incremental provision of more-sophisticated air cover and protection has been a hallmark of Soviet policy in Angola. Advanced SAM-6 antiaircraft missile and radar systems first appeared in southern Angola in 1981 and were knocked out by South Africa in Operation Protea. In the battle at Cuvelai, South African forces captured a SAM-9 intact for the first time. In addition, Moscow began training more Angolan pilots and supplying the more advanced MIG-23 and Sukhoi fighters to supplement the MIG-21, the backbone of Angola's air force.

Quasi War: The Battle of Lomba River

In December 1983 and January 1984, the Soviets decided to embark on a more assertive military strategy. In a major reassessment at a joint conference with the Cubans and Angolans, the USSR agreed to a massive resupply effort, to more sophisticated air defenses, and to deploying its advisers down to the battalion level rather than merely as staff at headquarters. Soviet officers actually were to command some artillery, air force, and armored units. In the eighteen-month period after the conference, the Soviet resupply effort included the counterinsurgency equipment shown in table 7.

For their part, the Cubans agreed to send units into combat in addition to their normal training and garrison duties. Although some Cubans troops had been killed when towns or military installations were attacked, as had some advisers, no Cuban troops had been committed as combat units between 1977 and 1983.[20] The agreement to deploy combat units represented a major new commitment on Cuba's part because, of course, significantly more casualties would be expected.

All this amounted to a new strategy designed to eliminate the UNITA insurgency rather than merely containing it and sallying forth from the cit-

TABLE 7
SOVIET GROUND ATTACK COUNTERINSURGENCY EQUIPMENT SUPPLIED
DURING 1984–1985

Equipment	Number supplied
MIG-23 fighter bombers	23
Su-22 fighter bombers	10
MIG-21 fighter bombers	17
MI-25 helicopter gunships	25

SOURCE: *Times* (London), September 24, 1985, p. 7.

adels. Instead of just fortifying the towns, the combined Soviet, Cuban, and Angolan forces, with the help of some East Germans who served primarily in communications, would prepare to attack the main insurgent stronghold in the remote Cuando Cubango region of southern Angola. What followed has been almost a small conventional war, one conducted each year since 1985 during the dry season.

UNITA's success in the Angolan provinces in 1983 threatened Soviet prestige, even though the possibility of overthrowing the MPLA was negligible.

The first and major test of this new strategy occurred in 1985, culminating in the battle of Lomba River, which took place between September 28 and October 3. After a slow, methodical advance across southern Angola, the combined Soviet, Cuban, and Angolan forces arrived at the Lomba River, the gateway to Jamba, UNITA's capital. The propaganda battle is hard fought over Angola, but Western diplomats generally accept the South African version of the battle, with some discounting for exaggeration of enemy strength.[21] The Angolan army had approximately 30 Soviet T-62 tanks and 80 other Soviet-made armored personnel carriers to support its eleven advancing brigades. These were constantly resupplied through a network of Soviet-built airfields, guarded by Soviet planes and an elaborate radar network constructed by the Soviets.

Between nine and fourteen Soviet advisers may have been with each battalion; none were killed because they were withdrawn by helicopter when things went badly.[22] The Soviets commanded most of the air force, artillery, and armored units.[23]

The Angolan army and its Soviet and Cuban allies, however, were unable to take UNITA's capital, and many Cubans were killed in what was basically a conventional battle. The Soviet-supported forces did drive UNITA forces out of an area of Angola next to Zaire in a second and lesser offensive, thus cutting off access to another source of support, but Savimbi has reopened this line of communication. Some Angolans claimed that had the Soviets advised the Angolans to pursue only one offensive, concentrating on the push to Savimbi's capital, success would have been forthcoming. Thus considerable friction ensued between the Angolans and their Soviet advisers.

In 1986 a similar, but less vigorous, offensive was launched after another major Soviet resupply effort. The caution observed in this offensive seemed to reflect in part the arrival of U.S. Stinger anti-aircraft missiles, which were not available at the Lomba River.

Confronting South Africa: The 1987 Offensive

In 1987 the Angolan government mounted an offensive of an entirely new character. Instead of seeking primarily to eliminate the UNITA insurgency, the offensive appeared to be aimed at South African targets. So many Soviet advisers appeared with each Angolan army brigade (70 to 90 by one probably exaggerated account) that they seemed to be taking on a combat function beyond mere advising. Soviet advisers were fighting along with Cubans, and a captured Angolan said there were six Soviet officers in the frontlines of his unit "down to the company" level.[24]

The Soviet Foreign Ministry admitted Soviet troops were manning much of the hardware with Angolan units, including tanks, helicopters, and ground-to-air missiles, but denied they were fighting as combat units. Cuban mechanized infantry and tank corps also participated, along with a Cuban combat unit.[25] Most important, Soviet, Cuban, and Angolan pilots reportedly engaged South African jets in dogfights, for the first time shooting down some of them.

The Angolans claimed that ten planes were shot down, including seven of South Africa's best, but South Africa claimed only one was partially damaged.[26] It was clear that Angolan pilots trained by Soviet instructors at Lubango were increasingly capable of challenging South African air superiority; however, Cubans had flown for some time. The evidence of Soviet pilots participating is substantial, including eyewitness reports and taped conversations of the pilots.[27]

The conflict began in July and culminated in November, with captured equipment and personnel being displayed by UNITA in mid-November (see table 8). The offensive was planned and monitored by the highest-ranking officer ever posted beyond the Soviet periphery (Eastern Europe and Af-

TABLE 8
SOVIET AND ALLIED EQUIPMENT AND PERSONNEL CAPTURED BY UNITA
IN 1987 OFFENSIVE

Equipment/Personnel	Number captured
T-55 tanks	20
SA-8 & SA-13 missiles	6
Cuban MIG-23 pilots	2
Other military vehicles	200

SOURCE: *Washington Post*, November 2, 1987, p. A17.

ghanistan), four-star General Konstantin I. Shaganovitch, with the aid of a counterinsurgency specialist, three-star General Mikhail A. Petrov.[28]

An estimated $1 billion in Soviet equipment arrived in the Angolan capital, Luanda, by Soviet AN-24 flights, as many as twelve per day over a six-month period.[29] Four IL-76 planes ferried supplies to the front.[30]

The eighteen-thousand-man Angola force included large numbers of Soviet advisers attached to each brigade to assure adherence to Soviet strategy. According to UNITA, 20 Cuban soldiers and 4 Soviet soldiers were killed, and 75 Cubans and 31 Soviets were wounded in the offensive. UNITA also claimed to have killed 125 Cuban soldiers and 4 Soviet soldiers in simultaneous guerrilla operations elsewhere in Angola.[31] Pretoria claimed that 120 Russians and Cubans were killed.[32]

Taking part in the drive were as many as 150 Soviet tanks supported by MIG-23s and Sukhoi SU-22s flying from a string of airfields protected by an elaborate Soviet radar and missile network. For the first time in Angola, the USSR deployed M-46 guns and the new Mi-35 derivative of the Mi-24 Hind helicopter. UNITA claimed to have destroyed seven Soviet T-55 tanks and nineteen armored vehicles and shot down one Mi-25 helicopter and at least two MIGs.[33]

The Soviet planes, piloted by Angolans, Cubans, and Soviets, repeatedly bombed and strafed UNITA positions at Mavinga until South Africa decided to deploy its Mirage fighters. At least one, and perhaps more, of these fighters was shot down, the first time South Africa admitted such a loss.[34]

Although the offensive had been widely viewed as a major setback for the Soviets because the Angolan forces did not capture key towns like Mavinga near the UNITA headquarters and their forces in the sixth military district were almost obliterated, some South African planes had been shot down, which suggests that their air superiority may have been tenuous. Given the magnitude of the commitment, the offensive represented a stunning defeat for Moscow, but within weeks reinforcements were on the way, culminating in the biggest land battle in the history of southern Africa.

Southern Africa's Biggest Battle

On November 7, 1987, the Angolan president met Fidel Castro in Moscow, where a decision was made to replace newly recruited Cuban troops in Angola with experienced men.[35] Angola's highest-ranking military officer stated that there would be no increase in Cuban troops, an exercise in duplicity since within six months up to fifteen thousand new troops arrived along with Cuba's best pilots.[36] The consultation in Moscow between Angola, Cuba, and the Soviets was reminiscent of a similar coordination in early 1984 after Operation Askari.[37] Despite continual reports of friction between them, what is notable is the close cooperation, especially in crises.

Normally the rainy season in southern Angola interrupts the annual offensive for several months, but immediately following the failure of the 1987 operation, Cuban reinforcements began to arrive, and the Angolan chief of staff threatened to attack South African troops. For the first time South Africa admitted being inside Angola to help the rebels in defending their capital, Jamba. The Angolan chief of staff was quoted as saying: "We cannot exclude the possibility of conflict between the Cuban troops and the South Africans."[38]

The Cuban reinforcements included the crack 50th Division, which was dispatched immediately to the war zone in southeast Angola. Command of the Cuban forces went to a decorated and experienced veteran, General Arnaldo Ochoa Sanchez, who held key positions in both Ethiopia and Nicaragua.[39] General Sanchez was a member of the Cuban Communist Party's Central Committee and a deputy defense minister who served in Angola in the initial intervention.[40]

On December 10, 1987, the Angolan president announced that he was authorizing Cubans to start patrolling down to the Namibian border to engage South African forces in direct conflict.[41] Shortly after that a *New York Times* reporter saw truckloads of Cubans moving around Lubango, Angola's southern military headquarters, along with numerous Soviet advisers.[42] Simultaneously, Vietnamese military advisers arrived in Luanda.[43]

What followed was the biggest land battle in the history of southern Africa, centering on two key Angolan air bases along the Soviet-manned air defense system in southern Angola. On January 13, 1988, UNITA and South African troops (Operation Hooper) attacked Cuito Cuanavale, the most easterly air base from which the annual offenses against Savimbi's capital had been launched.[44]

At this point Angolan duplicity and disinformation surfaced again. On February 26, Pedro de Castro Van Dunem, an Angolan cabinet minister, assured his listeners on BBC that Cuban troops were not in Cuito Cuanavale. Three weeks later, on March 17, the Cubans claimed that advisers had arrived as early as December 5, 1987, and troops by mid-January 1988.[45]

General Sanchez directed the defense from the Menongue air base immediately west of Cuito Cuanavale. Cuba's best pilots flew MIG-23 bombing and strafing missions from Menongue against the besieging forces.[46] ANC and SWAPO forces acted as scouts, and the defenders used mobile radar stored in underground bunkers to direct the Soviet planes and the Cuban-piloted Soviet attack helicopters.[47] The newly arrived North Vietnamese officers gave advice regarding methods to resist siege tactics.[48] Privately, Soviet strategists boasted of Cuito as "Angola's Stalingrad."[49] This extraordinary combination of Soviet clients was able to hold Cuito Cuanavale, despite massive bombardment, leaving a military stalemate in south-central Angola.[50] By June up to fifteen thousand fresh Cuban troops had arrived and pushed to the Namibian border in the southwest.

Conclusion

The USSR had been massively involved in Angola since 1975, and its presence has grown steadily in numbers and sophistication. Although there are undoubtedly multiple interlocking and overlapping motives for this, the counterinsurgency objective—protecting the Angolan government from the UNITA rebels—seemed to have been superseded by a new willingness to confront South Africa in what almost amounted to a conventional war. This greatly strengthened the Cuban side in the 1988 negotiations over Namibian independence and Cuban withdrawal from Angola[51] and was certainly a factor in bringing South Africa to the table. The costs of Soviet adventurism, however, had been raised dramatically by U.S. support for UNITA, which accounts in part for Soviet pressure on Cuba to be more flexible. Also the Cuban-MPLA forces suffered from Angola's weak infrastructure—local supplies were hard to get, repair facilities were inadequate—which caused morale problems among the Cubans, who were often deployed in rural areas. About one-fourth of the Cuban army was in Angola. These disenchanted Cuban soldiers often antagonized the local populace, making the counterinsurgency effort more difficult, and are known to have criticized Castro when they returned home. Also, the Marxist-Leninist policies further exacerbated Angola's multifarious economic problems. These costs and the risk of an escalating confrontation with the United States rendered Moscow more amenable to a diplomatic solution.

In spring 1989, Soviet defense minister Dmitri Yazov revealed that Angola was one of four countries in the Third World that are especially important to Soviet interests.[52] In early 1990 Soviet advisors, down to the battalion level, again participated with Cuban combat units in the annual offensive against UNITA. Cuba had stopped its troop withdrawal in violation of the 1988 accords; and another $800 million of Soviet military aid had arrived. Thus, despite the inability of the USSR and its clients to quash the insurgency, Moscow seemed determined to continue to play a strategic role in Angola. Angolan oil and diamond reserves are substantial, but above all its ports provide access to the South Atlantic.

The Soviet intervention in Angola demonstrates a whole new range of intentions and capabilities, which previously remained mere speculation and did not exist in the Congo crisis, and above all reflects the USSR's emergence as a global superpower capable of sustaining a major proxy military operation anywhere in the world.

6

MOZAMBIQUE

The USSR as Rear Guard

After serious setbacks in Mozambique during the Brezhnev regime, Mikhail Gorbachev seems to have settled on a subtle, long-range policy designed to strengthen the ruling party through a carefully calibrated aid program, while serving as the ultimate military rear guard. The objective is to improve the regime's ability to retain control of the "commanding heights" of political and economic policy. Although the Kremlin's innovative military strategy was the highlight of its involvement with Angola, its innovative foreign economic policy is the highlight of its involvement with Mozambique.

The successful insurgents in Mozambique (Frelimo) and Angola (MPLA) always had very different relationships with the USSR during the struggle for independence. Frelimo was never as close to the Soviets as the MPLA in Angola. Frelimo came to power in Mozambique without Cuban troops and with help from both China and the West.[1]

Frelimo was more resistant to Soviet blandishments from the beginning because it had experience in government, having ruled liberated zones for some time before taking power, which was not the case for the MPLA. At independence in June 1975, China's influence was probably greater than that of the USSR. In fact, the new foreign minister had warned the Soviets against interference in Mozambique's internal affairs.[2]

Soviet influence with Frelimo has fluctuated over the years since independence, reaching its high watermark in 1977 with the signing of a Friendship Treaty, then plummeting after the refusal of admission to the CMEA in 1980, and reaching its nadir in 1984 when Mozambique signed a pact with South Africa.

In the economic field, Mozambique is much more dependent on South Africa than is Angola. Mozambique sells electricity from the Cabora Bassa Dam to South Africa. It also supplies labor to South Africa, and South Africans have a stake in the port of the capital city, Maputo.

Since 1984 the Kremlin has unveiled a rather clever foreign economic policy designed to enhance Soviet influence while avoiding excessive costs and risks. For example, in 1985 the USSR, under the more vigorous and sophisticated Gorbachev, engineered an elaborate series of agreements between the CMEA—which facilitates trade and aid with the USSR and Eastern Europe, as well as Cuba and Vietnam—and Mozambique, thus helping dissipate the bad taste left by the refusal of full membership in CMEA early in the decade.[3] No other country in the region had such an arrangement.

Strategic Cooperation: A Rear Guard

In the strategic arena, Mozambique has consistently denied Moscow's requests for bases at the superb harbors along its 1,500-mile coast, although the USSR does use its ports to service the Soviet fleet. A Soviet dry dock was installed in 1981. Thus Soviet military involvement is limited to aid and training, but that involvement might escalate dramatically if the insurgency inside the country continues to gather strength or if the crisis in South Africa spills over.

At times the USSR has indicated a willingness to escalate its military involvement. In 1983 the USSR sent four warships and an aircraft carrier to Maputo for eight days.[4] In 1981, Moscow deployed a naval squadron including one cruiser and three smaller vessels after a South African raid, and the Soviet ambassador warned South Africa against such incursions.[5] One obscure report indicated that Soviet pilots flew Soviet planes in defense of Beira, the vital harbor that services Zimbabwe.[6]

In 1986 the Cubans offered to send an Angolan-style expeditionary force, and Soviet General Yevgeny Ivanovsky suggested ringing the capital, Maputo, with an advanced radar system.[7] There are still (1989) four hundred to six hundred Cuban military advisers (down from seven hundred to eight hundred in 1978) and perhaps five hundred to six hundred Cuban civilians. Castro has even suggested that Cuba will not leave Africa until apartheid is ended in South Africa, which suggests a continued willingness to escalate that nation's involvement should it be requested.[8]

However, both Frelimo and the USSR clearly fear a confrontation with the powerful South African military machine, which would be so near to its home bases, unlike the situation in Angola. Three Soviet leaders—Brezhnev, President Podgorny on a state visit to Maputo, and Andropov during Machel's visit to Moscow in 1983—warned the late President Samora Machel to do everything possible to avoid open conflict with South Africa. This may be one reason why Mozambique president Joaquin Chissano turned down the 1986 Cuban and Soviet offer of an expeditionary force. He is also known to be disillusioned with Soviet equipment and advice because of past experience.

The two hundred Soviet military advisers did a poor job of converting the Frelimo guerrilla army into a conventional force, and then the USSR provided an assortment of soon-to-be obsolete tanks, missiles, and planes. In 1983, after the Renamo guerrillas were operating freely almost everywhere in the country, the USSR did deliver a few sophisticated helicopter gunships.

Nevertheless, to assume that the USSR would not intervene militarily in Mozambique under any circumstances is unwise. The extensive strategic consultations between the two sides and the visits of high-ranking Soviet officers indicate that such intervention can hardly be ruled out. On at least two occasions major intervention was considered. The first instance occurred in June 1982, when General Alexei Yepishev, then chief of the Main Political Directorate of the Soviet army, toured the country after Mozambique's minister of defense had returned from talking in Moscow with his Soviet counterpart, Marshal Ustinov. The second instance occurred at President Machel's funeral in 1986. A 40-man Soviet delegation contained numerous military figures, including the aforementioned Marshal Ivanovsky. At present, the USSR provides a rear guard for Mozambique militarily, but given the volatility of its neighbor, this cannot be taken for granted.[9]

In the interim, Soviet-Cuban behavior reflects a carefully tailored long-range strategy to facilitate development by strengthening the party (Frelimo) through greater discipline and education. More than 6,500 Mozambicans have studied in Cuba. In 1987, eight hundred technical experts returned from Cuba, and four hundred students left for Cuba.[10] This finely calibrated approach to development represents a new Soviet foreign economic policy for Mozambique, one designed to correct past mistakes while enhancing Frelimo's grip on the "commanding heights" of policy.

TABLE 9
SOVIET AID TO MOZAMBIQUE

Years	Level of aid
1975–1977	$3 million
1977–1979	2 million
1982–1990	100 million[a]

SOURCE: FBIS-MEA 87-090, May 11, 1987.
[a]Mostly credits.

Mozambique: A Bellwether of Soviet Foreign Economic Policy

A dramatic signal of the USSR's intention to increase the relative importance of foreign economic policy in southern Africa was the multidimensional cooperative arrangement reached in January 1982 between Angola and the Soviet Union. It was the largest single financial commitment in Africa to date, estimated at $2 billion. It included a ten-year economic collaboration agreement and a more specific five-year trade, economic, and technical accord.[11]

A series of miscalculations and setbacks, particularly in Mozambique, probably provided the catalyst for this new foreign economic policy.[12] The Kremlin had provided only $3 million in economic aid to Mozambique by 1977, and another $2 million by 1979 (see table 9). Thus at the Third Party Congress of Frelimo in 1977, perhaps the high watermark of Soviet influence, Mozambique's president, Samora Machel, must have clearly perceived that aid from the USSR would not play as important a role in the development process as he had imagined.

Mozambique's subsequent experience reaffirmed this dramatically, particularly with the Kremlin's refusal to accept Machel's fervent appeals for admission to the CMEA in the early 1980s, despite the apparent support of the East Germans, who pressed hard for Mozambique's membership. The CMEA treaty, which establishes elaborate trade and aid mechanisms for Soviet-dominated communist states, calls for member states to help poor members reach levels of economic development equal to those of the more prosperous states. As one of the least developed countries in the world, Mozambique would have theoretically benefited enormously from CMEA membership.

In addition, despite the radical economic downturn after the imposition of

TABLE 10
SOVIET CREDITS AND GRANTS TO MOZAMBIQUE IN EARLY 1980s

1982	$5 million
1983	15 million
1984	5 million

SOURCE: U.S. Department of State: Warsaw Pact Economic Aid to Non-Communist Less-Developed Countries, 1984.

Marxist economic policies in the late 1970s and Machel's appeal for more help, the USSR did not respond with a substantial increase in aid and credits (see table 10), although it did seek to improve the terms of the credits offered.

Other aspects of Soviet aid further aggravated Soviet-Mozambique relations. The Soviets apparently required cash payment for technical services. Mozambique also discovered Soviet goods to be less attractive in terms of financing, service, quality, and delivery times. Another major irritant was the requirement that Soviet bloc trade and aid be transported by the Soviet merchant marine. This, plus careful rate slashing, has helped the Soviet bloc garner a substantial portion of the East African coastal shipping trade. The USSR's parsimonious attitude encouraged Machel to turn toward more capitalist methods at home and to look elsewhere for aid.[13]

Reacting to this, more pragmatic voices ultimately prevailed in the Kremlin, reflected in a ten-year economic agreement committing approximately $100 million for the 1980s. Various long-term mineral and infrastructural cooperation agreements implementing this commitment were signed during the third session of the Soviet-Mozambican Intergovernmental Commission for Economic and Technical Cooperation and Trade during April 1985, although it is not clear how much of this is in the form of credits and how much in grants.[14] Because Mozambique pays for its military aid, most is probably in the form of loans. Eleven large farming cooperatives comprised one of the major projects for which the $100 million was targeted. Although this $100 million represented a major new commitment to Mozambique, it appears paltry when compared to the $2 billion committed to Angola at the same time.

As part of this new economic initiative, the Kremlin also doubled its trade with Mozambique in 1984. Soviet-Mozambican trade had steadily increased since 1980 but began to fall in 1985 as the insurgency progressed (see table 11). The Soviet share of all Mozambican imports increased from 4.7 percent in 1982 to 19 percent in 1984. The USSR also continues to supply almost all of Mozambique's oil on easy-credit terms. In October 1985 a trade agreement for the period 1986–1990 was signed to further increase the value of trade between the two countries.[15]

Despite the improved credit terms and the increased value of the trade, the disparity between Soviet exports and Soviet imports is so substantial as to suggest exploitation. Table 11 indicates how advantageous this trade relationship is for the USSR, which dumps its comparatively shoddy goods on poverty-stricken Mozambique and ultimately milks Mozambique's scarce foreign exchange and its raw materials in payment for goods that by and large could be manufactured in Mozambique. Manufacturing in Mozambique would also preserve foreign exchange, allowing mineral exports to earn foreign exchange and improve the chronic unemployment situation.

The Post-Nkomati Foreign Economic Offensive

In 1985 Moscow sent another signal that it was developing a new foreign economic policy toward southern Africa when it orchestrated a major sale on credit to Mozambique of badly needed oil from Libya, Angola, and the USSR. The terms were apparently quite favorable. This was part of an orchestrated response to the famous March 1984 Nkomati Accords[16] between Mozambique and South Africa that stipulated neither side would help insurgents in their respective countries and laid the foundation for extensive economic cooperation.

Anticipating some sort of accommodation between Mozambique and

TABLE 11
SOVIET TRADE WITH MOZAMBIQUE 1977–1985
(IN MILLIONS OF RUBLES)

Year	Soviet Exports	Soviet Imports
1985	83.9	1.5
1984	137.5	1.6
1983	77.0	.8
1982	44.2	6.7
1981	35.7	1.3
1980	17.9	1.7
1979	20.3	.9
1978	17.4	.8
1977	5.9	—

SOURCE: Soviet Foreign Trade Statistics (Moscow), see Note 15.

South Africa, the Soviets mounted a skillfully conceived economic and propaganda offensive to mitigate its impact. In December 1983 the Soviet ambassador in the Mozambique capital, Maputo, demonstrated a new Soviet sophistication when he publicly declared that the USSR understood Mozambique's desire to improve its relations "in all directions" and that Mozambique was "nobody's puppet." Going further, the ambassador pointed to a $300 million trade agreement that had just been signed and announced that more shiploads of rice and oil would arrive. After a worldwide appeal by Frelimo in January 1984, just before the Nkomati Accords were signed, the USSR was the first creditor to agree to reschedule Mozambique's debt. The Kremlin was also the first to provide consumer goods for the agricultural marketing plan, including shipments of Soviet goods worth an estimated $13 million—clothing, domestic utensils, and an estimated 22,000 watches.

The most dramatic and unprecedented move involved food aid, which is not traditionally an instrument of Soviet foreign policy. Moscow sent 3,000 tons of fish to Mozambique in 1984, which is double the normal annual fish imports of that country. The fish gift may have been partially motivated by the desire to help erase Moscow's unsavory reputation for excessively exploiting the fishing grounds of its African clients. For example, in 1977 Angola received only 12 percent of the fish caught by the Russians in its waters, and the Kremlin's fishing vessels return only 25 percent of the catch in Mozambique's waters.

One reason the Soviets did not react more negatively to the Nkomati Accords is that Moscow has long accepted that development will require Western aid. In fact, the Kremlin regards Western aid as an obligation because of the economic retardation allegedly caused by colonial exploitation. What the USSR regards as paramount is that the party—in this case Frelimo—retain political control by controlling what Lenin called the "commanding heights" of the economy.

During late 1984, the USSR supplied Mozambique with consumer goods valued at $8 million to be bartered for agricultural goods produced by peasant farmers. It was announced that a similar donation valued at $11.7 million would be received in the last quarter of 1985.[17] Support for peasant farming also represents a shift in traditional Soviet policy from focusing exclusively on big state farms. In addition, the USSR announced that it would help with the irrigation of 200,000 hectares in the Limpopo Valley and the training of agricultural personnel. After a freak storm in Maputo, the Soviet ambassador was one of the first to announce aid to restore power lines and other infrastructural aspects. Credits of $4 million were extended to Mozambique.

At the third meeting of the Soviet-Mozambican Intergovernmental Commission for Economic and Technical Cooperation and Trade, held in

April 1985, a number of documents on economic cooperation were signed. Furthermore, Soviet spokesmen made promises of "concrete support to eliminate famine and armed bandits" during a visit to Mozambique in May 1985, which resulted in an $11.7 million grant of consumer goods to Mozambique. A similar grant ($14 million) had been made in 1984. A Soviet Afro-Asian Solidarity Committee delegation also visited Mozambique in December 1985 to present aid worth $500,000.

During 1986 the USSR continued to expand its economic activities. On the tenth anniversary of the first trade and economic agreements with Mozambique, the Soviet ambassador delivered an address that pointed specifically to those projects that the USSR considered most significant: Soviet assistance in the coal-mining venture at Moatze and in the rehabilitation of the railway line between Beria and Moatze (a $164 million project). He also pointed to the presence of 650 Soviet specialists working in various other fields in Mozambique. Other Soviet projects were the joint fishing company Moso Pesca, the installation of a floating dock for naval repairs, a study by the Soviet Union on the economic potential of the Limpopo Valley, Soviet assistance in the reopening of several small ports, educational projects, and provision of fuel supplies.

Economic Constraints: The CMEA Controversy

Mozambique's abortive attempt to gain admission to the CMEA, despite East German sponsorship, provides an example of the severe constraints on Soviet foreign economic policy in the region, as well as its ability to adapt to the specific situation. The CMEA includes only two Third World nations, Cuba and Vietnam, although both Mozambique and Angola have participated as observers. The CMEA treaty requires continuous efforts to "level up" the economies of member states, many of which are suffering economic dislocations. Apparently the burden of leveling up Cuba and Vietnam persuaded most East European states (excluding East Germany) to oppose Mozambique's admission. Moscow, whose influence is decisive, ultimately acquiesced in that opposition.

East Germany, having been delegated considerable responsibility for coordinating communist bloc activities in southern Africa, was naturally more concerned about Mozambique's desperate economic plight. Also, East Germany possesses the most prosperous economy in the Soviet bloc and thus would have been better able to endure the leveling process. Finally, East Germany viewed its activities in Africa as a means of legitimizing its international status. For a time, East Germany was more closely integrated with Mozambique than any African country with any communist state. East Germany will likely continue to press Mozambique's case with the CMEA secretariat, but success is not imminent, especially under the cost-conscious Gorbachev regime. Nevertheless, continued East German involvement with Mozambique is suggested by rumors of a substantial East German commitment to rehabilitate Mozambique's railroads.

Reacting to its rejected bid to join the CMEA, Mozambique turned to the West for aid, joined the Lome Convention and the International Monetary Fund, and opened relations with West Germany. Its West German move was a direct slap at East Germany, a major trading partner that accounted for 8.1 percent of Mozambique's exports and 5.5 percent of its imports in 1980.

The Gorbachev regime has adopted an innovative and finely tuned approach to mitigate the damage to the Soviet image caused by the CMEA episode by initiating a series of agreements between Mozambique and the CMEA. On May 22, 1986, Mozambique became the first southern African country to sign an economic cooperation and development agreement and to form a joint commission with the CMEA. The agreement covers agriculture, industry, geology, health, and education.[18] In his closing speech to the People's Assembly in July 1986, Machel referred to the CMEA agreement as an "important step forward" in Mozambique's relations with "other socialist countries which are a firm support in our fight for peace and development."[19]

In short, although the USSR does not regard Mozambique either economically or politically as a candidate for full membership in the "socialist commonwealth" like genuine communists (for example, Cuba and Vietnam), it is nevertheless concerned enough to bind Mozambique to that commonwealth as much as possible without undertaking the enormous burden inherent in leveling up. This is a good example of the USSR's increasing ability to fine-tune its foreign economic policy.

Economic Constraints on Soviet Influence

Soviet activity in Mozambique reflects a highly selective effort to attenuate, if not offset, the impact of Western and even Chinese influence.[20] Moscow had given Mozambique 17,000 tons of grain in 1982 and 10,000 tons in 1983. The Soviet Union's combined gift of fish and grain make it a food donor equal to each of Mozambique's other major donors—the United States, the EEC, and Holland, all of which pledged 30,000 to 45,000 tons of grain in 1984 and a similar quantity in 1985. The appearance of parity with the United States has been a major objective of Soviet foreign policy for some time. This is one instance of the USSR carefully fostering that image.

Of course, the United States and South Africa are capable of providing much more aid, as well as trade. In August 1984, South Africa promised a $6 million loan for developing Maputo's harbor and Mozambique's railroad service. The United States has pledged to step up assistance and took Mozambique off the aid blacklist shortly after the Nkomati Accords were signed.

Increased Chinese involvement in Africa often presages increased Soviet involvement because the USSR is acutely sensitive to ideological competition with its giant communist rival. In August 1982, Mozambique concluded its first trade agreement with China, thus reviving an important pre-independence connection. President Machel's visit to China in July 1984 was successful. He met the Chinese president and premier during the six-day visit. China offered him $13 million in soft-credit loans, repayable over ten years without interest, and $2 million in consumer goods.

Not to be outdone by Beijing, the Soviets promised in August 1984, immediately after Machel's China visit, to deliver substantially more fuel to Mozambique, suggesting that they intended to compete with China in foreign economic policy in southern Africa.

To keep these Soviet initiatives in perspective, one must remember that Mozambique has always been primarily part of the Western economic orbit. Even when Soviet influence was at its height in the late 1970s, 80 percent of Mozambique's exports went to the non-Soviet world. In 1986 Western economic assistance amounted to more than $500 million, while the USSR provided only about $5 million.[21]

By 1987, Mozambique had reached agreement with the International Monetary Fund, was privatizing its industry and agriculture, was encouraging foreign investment, and was reducing the number of communist advisers in mining. Since 1984 at least 30 firms in the light-industry sector have been privatized. In agriculture the government converted large Soviet-style state farms to private ones. In the crucial mining sector the number of communist advisers dropped from a high of 2,000 to 750.[22]

Nevertheless, Frelimo is still clearly in control of the "commanding heights," even though in August 1989 the first national party congress in five years endorsed some elements of free market economics. On March 11, 1987, the USSR and Mozambique signed a protocol that represented the outcome of a session of the Mozambique-USSR Joint Economic Commission. It covered at least three major areas of cooperation and assistance—rehabilitation of the state petroleum enterprise, rehabilitation of the Beira railroad corridor, and contributions to various industrial enterprises—and was apparently not a new commitment of resources but the implementation of the 1982 agreements.[23] Thus, although the USSR cannot compete with the West's economic power, it is continually adapting its foreign economic policy in Mozambique. The objective is to maximize the influence derived from its foreign economic policy while continually encouraging the vanguard party to maintain its political grip on the economy.

Whither Moscow and Maputo?

In summary, what does Soviet behavior tell us about Moscow's strategy in Mozambique? The Kremlin has recovered well from a serious but not devastating series of setbacks in a country where its influence was never as great as rhetoric in Moscow and Maputo portrayed. Gorbachev is content with normal, almost traditional, relations while blaming the setbacks on the previous regimes in the USSR and Mozambique. His economic aid program is limited, but relatively sophisticated, and designed to project an image of substantial commitment to development. However, it is carefully tailored to avoid major overcommitments like the leveling up inherent in CMEA membership. Moscow recognizes that this development process will indeed be long and that it cannot compete with the West economically. It is also wary of conflict with the powerful South African military machine, which explains why the Cubans carry the main burden of communist military aid on the ground.

Because Moscow is concerned about the party's control of the commanding heights of the economy, it concluded a party-to-party agreement. The Mozambique government has dramatically miscalculated in dealing with its ethnic divisions, and the Kremlin views a more disciplined party as a correction to this. Moscow, however, has always underestimated the strength of ethnic ties, and a stronger party alone is unlikely to resolve ethnic conflict.

Like the MPLA in Angola, Frelimo confronts a major insurgency (Renamo). In both nations, the central governments and ruling parties are weak at the local level, where communications are poor, arms caches easily hidden, and ethnic dissensions endemic.

In conclusion, the great imponderable in Mozambique's future is its security problem, which could provide the USSR with opportunities, although the risks are substantial. The Renamo rebels operate with relative impunity in most of the country. The Soviet counterinsurgency program has proved a failure. Maputo has rejected use of Cuban combat troops and an improved Soviet air-defense system. Nevertheless, the USSR has an interest in protecting access to the minerals of Mozambique and to its superb harbors. Under present circumstances, as in the past, the USSR would probably demand a base as a quid pro quo for any major new military support, and the regime in Maputo is even more likely to reject such a request than in the past. In

June 1989, Mozambique announced that Soviet military advisers would be cut from fifteen hundred to seven hundred and that the Cubans would be cut by 40 percent, but that helicopters and light military equipment would continue to flow. This could change, however, if the crisis in South Africa escalates. With its veterans returned from major counterinsurgency experiences in Afghanistan and with the extensive experience of the Soviet military advisers in Mozambique and Angola, Moscow is well positioned to take advantage of opportunities as they arise.

7

THE NONALIGNED STATES

Constraints and Opportunities

The USSR has been dramatically increasing its involvement in the region's nonaligned states throughout the decade while attempting to consolidate its hold on the insurgencies and its Afro-Marxist clients.

Although the program of the 27th Party Congress barely mentions Moscow's Afro-Marxist allies, focusing instead on other states in the Third World (even capitalist ones), this should not be interpreted as a strategic retreat.[1] The escalating involvement in the nonaligned states represents an effort to enhance the Kremlin's influence in other arenas in the region where there are new opportunities involving less cost and less risk. The new initiatives toward the nonaligned states reflect a general realization by Moscow that socialist development in Africa is slowed by ethnicity or what the Soviets term *special characteristics,* and, therefore, socialist development will take much longer than originally anticipated.

As Gann and Duignan pointed out earlier, "The Marx-Leninist republics have not surmounted the problems of ethnicity."[2] These new approaches by the Soviets do not represent a new strategy, as Richard Lowenthal observed some time ago. He argued that the Soviet Union has begun to move from old-style anti-imperialism to a new concept of counterimperialism: "a strategy of fighting Western imperialism by using the *familiar* methods of establishing zones of political and economic influence linked to the Soviet Union by firm ties."³

The essential Soviet tactics, as Richard Bissell astutely observed, involve "playing so many cards at the same time that there will generally be a gain in every loss."⁴ As Robert H. Jackson put it, "Soviet involvement in African affairs has been eclectic and expedient."⁵ The following describes and analyzes Soviet behavior in the region's nonaligned states, focusing particularly on the constraints and opportunities in each state.

Zambia: Instability as Opportunity

In its foreign policy, Zambia has always tilted slightly toward the West and has occasionally openly denounced Soviet intervention in southern Africa. However, because it served as the headquarters of the Soviet-backed "national liberation" movements, Zambia has always been central to Soviet involvement in the region. The main ANC office in Africa is there, and ZAPU, the unsuccessful Soviet-backed organization that opposed the white Rhodesian regime, was based there.

As a result, it is not surprising that Zambia's capital, Lusaka, houses the largest Soviet embassy in the region. Its staff of 129 includes 50 known KGB and GRU officers and an estimated 28 intelligence personnel with diplomatic cover.⁶ During the Rhodesian insurgency in the 1970s, Soviet ambassador Vasily Solodovnikov, allegedly a professional KGB officer, coordinated Soviet policy in the region. The presence of so many covert operatives is not always advantageous. In 1978 a furious Zambian president expelled some of them.⁷ Nevertheless, their numbers are likely to grow as the ANC escalates its activities inside South Africa.

The USSR concluded a major arms deal with Zambia in 1979–1980, during which time the Soviets delivered $180 million in arms, approximately 70 percent of Zambia's total arms imports. The arms sent included the MIG-21 fighter, SA-3 missiles, radar equipment, tanks, and armored personnel carriers.⁸ About five hundred Soviet military personnel were in Zambia training its defense forces.

In the early 1980s this military cooperation did not seem to translate into any significant political influence; President Kaunda pursued his basic policy of nonalignment and attempted to mediate a settlement in Namibia (the Lusaka Accord). He also negotiated with the South African government, contrary to Soviet interests at the time.

Nevertheless, the USSR pressed forward with enhanced political ties. The standard Friendship Society was established in the capital, and a formal party-to-party agreement between the CPSU and the ruling party of Zambia was concluded in May 1981. This was followed by several visits of delegations from each ruling party to the USSR and Zambia, respectively.[9] Party-to-party ties help Moscow identify rising young leaders and facilitate Soviet efforts to strengthen the indigenous party.

The USSR's inability to extract political capital from its initiatives in Zambia in the early 1980s probably reflects the heightened sense of security resulting from the end of the Rhodesian insurgency, when Soviet-backed guerrillas based in Zambia were often attacked. However, this is changing in several respects.

Above all, the ANC's increasing activities have led to South African raids into Zambia, and the Angolan civil war was spilling over into western Zambia (UNITA forces were occasionally driven into the area). At the same time, the faltering Zambian economy required cutbacks in Zambia's military.[10] This instability provides opportunities for new Soviet initiatives for which Moscow has laid a solid foundation based on long experience.

Nevertheless, Soviet sophistication should not be overestimated. In May 1987 the USSR appointed a new ambassador, Oleg Miroshkin, a former party secretary from the Soviet central Asian republic of Kazakhstan, where riots demonstrated that Gorbachev's policy in this developing area lacked a sensitivity to ethnicity, among other things.[11] If this means that the central Asian model is still Moscow's framework for analyzing the region, then further setbacks are predictable in this geographically and politically central state.

Botswana: Democracy as Constraint

For such a weak country economically and politically, Botswana has achieved some measure of economic prosperity; it is also one of the few successful functioning democracies in the region.[12] Both its economic and its political achievements as well as its proximity to South Africa's military power—in Namibia on its western and northern borders, as well in South Africa proper on its southern border—severely constrain potential Soviet influence. As a result, the USSR has opted for more limited and traditional approaches.

The party-to-party approach is appropriate only for one-party states like Zambia. For a multiparty democracy like Botswana, Moscow relies more on state-to-state relations. So in May 1987 the USSR concluded its first trade agreement with Botswana.[13] Each nation will set up a trade mission in the other country and abide by the rules of most-favored-nation status. Trade will be conducted on a convertible-currency basis rather than barter, as is often the case in Soviet trade with Third World countries.[14]

Botswana's capital, Gaborone, provides the best access to the industrial heartland of South Africa of any adjacent state. Thus, it is an important staging area for the ANC, as well as a valuable listening post. The KGB certainly keeps in touch with ANC cadres there. In 1985, Moscow enlarged its embassy in Botswana, apparently largely for intelligence purposes, but also undoubtedly to aid the ANC. These covert operations will be facilitated by an estimated 28 KGB and GRU personnel in an embassy of 53.[15] This is not the first espionage scare in Botswana. After the USSR established diplomatic relations in 1978, it was thought that the KGB was involved in major covert operations, but this proved to be somewhat exaggerated.[16]

The Kremlin has also reportedly made generous offers of military assistance to Botswana in the mid-1980s.[17] Previously, from 1979 to 1983, the USSR accounted for fully 50 percent of Botswana's arms imports, including armored personnel carriers and SA-7 missiles, among others. Deputy Defense Minister Ian Khama, son of the first president, negotiated these sales in Moscow in 1981, so there has been significant arms cooperation with the Soviets.[18]

Nevertheless, the chief barrier to Soviet influence in this fragile nation is South African military power. In June 1985 and May 1986, South African commandos staged raids against ANC facilities near the capital with impunity. The fate of weak states like Botswana rests very much with this regional power, despite Soviet initiatives.

Lesotho: South African Power as Constraint

The significance of South African power as a constraint on Soviet influence, particularly in small states, is nowhere better illustrated than in the tiny, landlocked nation of Lesotho, which is entirely surrounded by South Africa. Despite major initiatives in the early 1980s, the USSR suffered a serious setback when the government of Chief Lebua Jonathan was ousted by a coup in January 1986.

In May 1985 for the first time the USSR named an ambassador for Lesotho alone. Previously the Soviet ambassador to Mozambique served Lesotho also. However, since 1962, an underground communist party served the USSR inside Lesotho, providing aid to the ANC cadres there. To counter this, South African commandos occasionally raided Lesotho to eliminate

ANC activities. The South African government also employed an array of economic carrots and sticks to influence the leader, Chief Jonathan.

Nevertheless, in 1983 the chief began to woo the USSR, apparently in an effort to attract international attention and aid. The Kremlin responded dramatically to these overtures with the full gamut of its instruments of foreign policy. Signaling the long-range commitment of the USSR to the region, one of the first acts was the departure of 38 students for the Soviet Union in late August 1983, although this was not announced at the time and was only acknowledged by Chief Jonathan a year later.[19]

In June 1984 a Soviet delegation, led by a member of the State Committee for Foreign Economic Relations, visited Maseru, the capital city, to explore prospects for economic and technical cooperation. In August the USSR and Lesotho signed an agreement on media cooperation.[20] A similar agreement was signed with Zimbabwe, again reflecting Moscow's increasing emphasis on public diplomacy.

In September 1984 at the invitation of the Soviet Committee for Solidarity with Asian and African Countries, a large delegation, including the secretary general of the ruling Basotho National Party and Foreign Minister Vincent Makhele, visited Moscow for talks with Soviet officials.[21] In December, Makhele returned to Moscow to sign two agreements, a cultural and scientific accord and a technical and economic accord.

While it was taking these first steps toward party-to-party ties, media cooperation, and scientific, cultural, technical, and economic ties, the Kremlin was also increasing its covert capability, as indicated by the rather dramatic increase in its embassy staff to approximately 32.[22] Simultaneously, South Africa stepped up its pressure, primarily by supporting the Lesotho Liberation Army, an insurgency against Chief Jonathan reportedly based in South Africa. In January 1986 a coup eliminated Jonathan's regime and with it most of the Soviet gains. Major General Justin Lekanya, the new military ruler, canceled most of the agreements with the USSR.

Nevertheless, under the new Soviet ambassador, Boris Asoyan, an African expert, the USSR continues to use Lesotho as a listening post, for example, by meeting South Africans of all races who travel to Maseru, the capital. Of course, the excessively large embassy staff and its bloated intelligence contingent remain.

Lesotho illustrates how quickly the USSR can take advantage of opportunities in southern Africa. In three years it was able to employ the full range of its foreign policy instruments, except the military one. Despite the setback represented by the coup, Moscow remains in a far better position in Lesotho than it did when the decade began. The king—primarily a figurehead, but highly respected by the people—and two of the ministers are still reportedly very close to the ANC.[23]

Zimbabwe: Insecurity as Opportunity

Whereas Lesotho represents a clear setback for Soviet policy in the region, Zimbabwe provides an important illustration of Soviet resilience after a major policy debacle. The USSR backed the wrong horse in the struggle for Zimbabwe's independence and was apparently surprised by Robert Mugabe's ultimate victory, achieved despite Moscow's massive commitment to Mugabe's rival insurgent leader, Joshua Nkomo. When the USSR was excluded from the Lancaster House talks, which led to independence, the Kremlin asked its client, Nkomo, to boycott them, but he refused even this. Soviet influence was at its nadir, and Moscow was not represented at the independence ceremony.[24]

Nevertheless, the USSR has gradually attempted to expand its influence in the face of profound mistrust by the regime. Events may favor Soviet initiatives. Zimbabwe faces crises on every border, as well as internal dissension. Its economy has been reasonably strong, but the slowly deteriorating security situation provides the USSR with opportunities. One such instance is reflected in the rumors of negotiations aimed at supplying the Zimbabwe air force with MIG-29s, which, because they are capable of competing with the best South African aircraft, threaten the air superiority so vital to South Africa's preponderance of military power in the region.[25] Of course, there is still some question about the quality and training of pilots and maintenance personnel.

Ignoring the folly of the Kremlin's decision makers during the insurgency, some Soviet political analysts viewed Zimbabwe in a favorable light from independence day onward. They identified it as being in the early stages of evolution toward full socialist orientation, largely because of its anti-imperialism and self-professed Marxism. Zimbabwe refused to denounce the Soviet downing of a Korean airliner. Also, one of its officials publicly insulted former President Carter and U.S. diplomats at a party in the capital, Harare, in 1986.[26]

Going further, Zimbabwe sponsored a U.N. resolution that condemned the U.S. operations in Grenada, thus facilitating a major public diplomacy offensive for the USSR throughout the world.[27] In 1986, as head of the nonaligned movement, President Mugabe orchestrated an attack on U.S. Africa policy, an attack that again was given worldwide publicity by the Soviet media and associated fronts. By this time the United States had cut its aid to Zimbabwe—to the obvious satisfaction of the Soviets, if not President Mugabe.[28]

Ideologically even at independence Zimbabwe showed signs of developing a political and economic system more compatible with the USSR. Nevertheless, it took almost a year for Moscow to establish diplomatic relations, and even then President Mugabe demanded a clause in the treaty of recognition promising that Soviet diplomats would not interfere in the internal affairs of his country. This reflects his pre-independence experience with the USSR, as well as the experience of most states in the region with the KGB, whose presence is still multiplying.[29]

In 1981 the new prime minister toured Eastern Europe, but avoided the Soviet Union. However, in 1983 a deputy head of the International Department of the CPSU visited Harare. As a result Zimbabwe, like Lesotho, established a Tass link allegedly as part of an effort to balance news coverage from East and West. Because Tass is well known for harboring intelligence operatives, this gave Moscow an opportunity to enhance its public diplomacy offensive and its covert capability in Zimbabwe.

At this time the USSR managed the two disinformation events described earlier (see chapter 1). The Tass link certainly facilitated these capers, and it also helped the Soviets exploit differences between the United States and the USSR, specifically by providing massive coverage of the reduction of U.S. economic aid to Zimbabwe after it abstained from the U.N. vote condemning Moscow for shooting down the Korean airliner.[30]

What followed the Tass agreement was a series of visits to Moscow by the top Zimbabwean leaders: the speaker of the House of Assembly (in 1983), the president (in 1984 and 1987), and Prime Minister Mugabe himself (in 1985). At a lower level, in 1983 Soviet trade union leaders opened up regular contacts with their Zimbabwean counterparts. In 1984 a large Soviet delegation attended the ruling party's congress in Zimbabwe, setting the stage for the inevitable party-to-party agreement.[31] In January 1984, Zimbabwe and the USSR concluded their first trade and economic cooperation accord. In February 1985, Zimbabwe finally sent its first ambassador to Moscow, making it possible for Mugabe's important visit.

In December 1985 Mugabe traveled to Moscow to meet Mikhail Gorbachev and sign several accords. They met for three hours and reportedly got along well. Mugabe signed the expected party-to-party agreement, as Zambia, Lesotho, Mozambique, and Angola had done previously. He also concluded an economic and cultural agreement. Perhaps even more significantly, he also reportedly met Konstantin Katushev, who handled Soviet arms sales to the Third World.[32] The previous September, Western intelligence reported the arrival of some twenty Soviet T-54 tanks. This was the first sign of potential military cooperation.[33]

All this took place as the security situation, both internally and externally, deteriorated. The introduction of Zimbabwean troops into counterinsurgency operations inside Mozambique led to the insurgents retaliating inside Zimbabwe. In Matabeleland dissidents stirred up trouble, which may be less serious now that Nkomo and Mugabe have achieved a rapprochement, although some dissident forces remain. Ironically, the absorption of Moscow's old client, Nkomo, by the ruling party may provide unusual opportunities for the USSR to exercise greater influence on it from within. Finally and most important, the South African crises have spilled over into Zimbabwe, with the South Africans allegedly encouraging the dissidents and with South African commando raids on Harare, thus exacerbating the security situation.

During this period the number of Soviet embassy staff grew from 48 to 62, including the usual complement of intelligence officers, 18 KGB and GRU with cover and 4 without—a third of the staff.[34]

In this context, an ominous rumor began circulating that the USSR had concluded an agreement to sell the advanced MIG-29 aircraft to Zimbabwe.[35] As described previously, a hallmark of Soviet policy in the region has been the gradual introduction of sophisticated military equipment, particularly in Angola. The introduction of the MIG-29 would represent a quantum leap because it could potentially threaten the air superiority so critical to South Africa's military dominance in the region.

The planes never arrived, and there are several proposed explanations. One is that discussions of such a purchase did take place, but that no agreement was reached. Another explanation is that the cost, a reputed $324 million, was too exorbitant for President Mugabe. Of course, it is also quite costly to service such modern aircraft and to train the pilots. Both arguments probably contain some germ of truth.

In April 1987, Zimbabwe's minister of defense denied in parliament that such planes had been purchased, but he did not deny discussing the possibilities of doing so. His air force chief had visited Moscow the previous month with a high-powered delegation. The most plausible explanation is that Mugabe decided that purchasing only twelve planes (as rumored) would actually damage Zimbabwe's security because it would provoke South African commando operations, but not be substantial enough to provide the superiority that might deter such raids.

There is no doubt that the USSR is pushing sales of the MIG-29 to such countries as Jordan, which is also in the frontline in a crisis area, to earn hard currency as well as to strengthen its diplomatic and political clout in the region. However, Mugabe has demonstrated a sensitivity to the risks of escalating Soviet involvement. As his insurgency approached its successful climax in 1979, he refused a Soviet-Cuban offer to set up a liberated zone, fearing that it would attract major South African involvement. What is certain is that Zimbabwe and the USSR have begun a major dialogue on security matters, which is the significance of the March 1987 visit to the USSR of Zimbabwe's minister of state for security, the air marshal, and the minister of state for political affairs.

Where this dialogue will lead depends to a considerable extent on developments in South Africa, but Soviet prospects are not as dim as they were at independence in 1980. Soviet economic specialists view Zimbabwe's development as more promising than that of war-torn Angola and Mozambique, which is why the minister of finance, economic planning, and development accompanied the March 1987 delegation, which discussed security. Soviet foreign policy has recovered after its disastrous support for ZAPU, the losing rebel group now part of the ruling party after having been in opposition since independence.

Moscow is moving on all fronts in Zimbabwe. For the USSR under Gorbachev, both Zimbabwe's relative economic success and its insecurity provide significant opportunities, and Soviet initiatives appear designed to take advantage of them. As the most prosperous nonaligned state in the region, Zimbabwe may eventually decide to purchase advanced weapons like the MIG-29.

Zaire: Traditional and Coercive Diplomacy

Throughout the 1980s the USSR has been quietly resuming normal relations with Zaire, which has always had closer ties to the West than any other black state in the region. It is also the most capitalist black state in the region.[36] The Soviet initiatives reflect the general conclusions embodied in Gorbachev's new party program, which calls for approaches to capitalist states in the Third World, not just Marxist or nonaligned states.[37]

Nevertheless, a cloud hangs over this new Soviet opening to Zaire: the continuing enmity between Zaire and Moscow's client Angola, which for the third time over the last decade or so seriously threatens to destabilize Zaire.[38] Again, the USSR seems to be involved in a double game of carrying on traditional relations while facilitating destabilization. A brief excursion into the previous history of Soviet involvement with Zaire may shed some light on the potential future development of relations between the two countries.

In the 1960s the USSR suffered a significant foreign policy defeat in Zaire when its clients were utterly defeated in the post-independence contest for power, which caused a major reassessment of Soviet African policy and concluded, like Gorbachev's recent reappraisal, that a breathing spell, *peredyshka*, was required while a more aggressive long-range plan was implemented.[39]

Zaire, with its great mineral wealth, is strategically positioned between the heartland of southern Africa and the Francophone countries, which have historically been anticommunist. Thus it is not surprising that Zaire supported the anticommunist side in the Angolan civil war. In fact, in 1965 a small Cuban contingent led by Ernesto "Che" Guevara fought with rebels against the newly independent government. This force was supplied by a flow of Soviet and Chinese arms funneled through Algeria and Egypt.[40]

A little over a decade later, in 1977 and 1978, Zaire's Shaba province, rich in copper and cobalt, was invaded unsuccessfully from Angola twice by Zairian dissidents, trained by Cubans and supplied with Soviet weapons. In the 1977 invasion the U.S. embassy reported that two thousand Cubans were poised to support the invaders and that the invaders were officered by Cubans.[41]

In 1978 there was evidence of East German involvement in such destabilization attempts. Berlin reportedly agreed to provide the invading force with military equipment that included a strike capacity against the weak Zairian air force. In 1977 a large number of heavy-duty Czech military transports were delivered, and one hundred East Germans trained the dissidents.[42] One report stated that it was clearly understood that the East Germans would not get involved directly.[43]

In the 1978 invasion, which seized the important mining town of Kolwezi, some evidence indicated that a puppet government would be installed should the rebels succeed. Antoine Gizenga, an old Soviet protégé from the post-independence power struggle, was brought to northern Angola along the border of Zaire, where he could easily have crossed to join the Angolan-backed rebels to claim the leadership of the country.[44]

Immediately before the invasion the USSR sent transports to buy huge quantities of cobalt, which they resold at enormous profits after the fighting disrupted production and panicked the world markets, all of which suggests Soviet complicity at the very least.[45]

Of course, both invasions failed when the Western powers sent troops to aid Zaire, but these two experiences and the Guevara one in 1965 bear attention, especially because UNITA is operating in the north and being supplied from Kamina, inside Zaire.

Naturally, relations between Zaire and the USSR plummeted after the two Shaba episodes until the early 1980s, when discreet contacts and exchanges facilitated a modest rapprochement.

The USSR often signals a new diplomatic offensive with an exchange of parliamentary delegations. In May 1981, Supreme Soviet deputies visited the capital, Kinshasa, and in August a legislative group from Zaire visited Moscow.[46] Almost two years later, in January and February of 1983, a Soviet trade union delegation visited the capital for a week and signed a joint communiqué on future cooperation with its counterpart, the Unions Nationale des Travailleurs du Zaire.[47] As in Zimbabwe, this constituted the second phase of the process. In April 1983 the two countries concluded what is normally the third stage of such an initiative: an agreement on cultural and scientific affairs.

Things seemed to be proceeding nicely in December 1983 when an agreement on marine cooperation was signed. But then fate intervened: in January 1984 an Aeroflot package blew up, accidentally destroying part of Kinshasa's airport. As a result until mid-1986 Soviet initiatives were confined to donating vaccines for tropical diseases. However, at that time the parties began to discuss the next phase of the process, economic and trade ties; and by the summer of 1987 party-to-party ties and other bilateral cooperation prospects were on the table when another Supreme Soviet delegation visited Kinshasa.[48]

Conclusion: A Pattern of Penetration

Although Moscow does not have a master plan for penetrating the moderate states of southern Africa, its activities reflect a relatively standard pattern of behavior designed to maximize its influence. First, the Kremlin sends low-level delegations, like Supreme Soviet deputies or trade-union representatives, and then cultural and scientific accords are negotiated. After this, the Soviets seek to conclude trade and aid agreements. Ultimately, with the one-party states the USSR strives for party-to-party relations. As Lowenthal put it, "zones of influence" are created. Finally, if there is a significant security problem, the Soviets offer security assistance in the form of training, advisers, and weapons, which are usually sold for hard currency. If the security situation continues to deteriorate, given its unique and considerable military experience in the region, Moscow's involvement is likely to grow substantially.

8

COERCIVE DIPLOMACY

*Tactics
and Instruments*

Despite four major offensives in the mid-1980s, including the massive Cuban rapid deployment of 1988, Moscow and its clients were unable to dictate a military solution in Angola and Namibia. The costs of Soviet adventurism had been raised dramatically. After the failure of its coercive diplomacy, Moscow maneuvered to avoid the perception that it was an unreliable patron pursuing a general geostrategic retreat under military pressure. In the wake of the Afghan debacle and a persistent U.S. diplomatic initiative combined with support for the UNITA insurgents, the USSR pressured Cuba and Angola to be more flexible at the bargaining table.[1] Cuba and the USSR (as an observer) came to the bargaining table because of forceful resistance to their domination of Angola, which had disenfranchised a large proportion of the population in the eyes of important African countries and the United States. Fifty-one U.S. senators signed a letter calling for UNITA participation in the government of Angola, while Nigeria, the Ivory Coast, Zaire, and Morocco, among others, acted behind the scenes to enfranchise UNITA and promote national reconciliation.

Throughout 1988 the United States and the USSR engaged in an intense dialogue at the summit, ministerial, and expert levels and were in daily contact as the November 1 deadline for the beginning of the Namibian independence process approached and passed.[2] The magnitude of the Soviet subventions to Cuba and Angola suggested that the USSR had considerable leverage with both these parties concerning their separate negotiations with South Africa and that neither could be regarded as independent actors.

Also during the year, Soviet officials hinted at proposals that offered hope for a resolution of the Angolan civil war. The USSR indicated that withdrawal of U.S. support to UNITA was not a precondition to settlement and further hinted that Jonas Savimbi might be part of a federal solution in which the south might have relative autonomy under his rule.[3]

In November 1988 after talking with Gorbachev and Aleksander Yakovlev, the Angolan president hinted for the first time at the possibility of Savimbi's being part of a settlement.[4] This followed upon the recognition of Savimbi's legitimacy by major African states and many U.S. senators, moves that retard the public diplomacy value of Soviet support for the minority Angolan regime.[5]

Thus some groundwork had been laid for national reconciliation, but Cuban withdrawal from Angola and South African withdrawal from Namibia remained obstacles. The latter was difficult to achieve, especially because of the perception among an increasingly conservative, white South African electorate that a likely SWAPO takeover in Namibia would encourage and facilitate the growing militancy of the ANC inside South Africa.

Although a withdrawal timetable had been worked out, the detailed procedures for verification and monitoring of this rather extended process left considerable room for a breakdown and in September 1989 Castro threatened to delay the Cuban pullout. A less complex, but somewhat similar, process rapidly disintegrated in 1984, although the United States and the USSR were not so intimately involved. For example, as the lengthy peace process unfolded, both the United States and the USSR hinted at joint sanctions should South Africa renege on its commitments. The prospect of a rapid Cuban redeployment must also have served to deter second thoughts in South Africa.

The gravity of the situation was reflected in the magnitude of Soviet-Cuban prestige involved as well as the enormity of the South African stake. South Africa could not appear to have lost a guerrilla war in Namibia, and Moscow could not appear to be withdrawing from southwestern Africa under military pressure as part of a general geostrategic retreat. Diplomats had to maneuver within these parameters.

The USSR, then, tends to view negotiations and a peace process as the beginning, not the end, of an ongoing struggle for influence. In Soviet eyes the 1988 accord on Namibia and Angola was the opening of a continuing competitive process. Soviet coercive diplomacy in southern Africa has revealed an extraordinary array of devices for projecting power in a carefully orchestrated way, which could surface in some form again if the peace process falters, if the MPLA begins to lose its grip, or for a number of other reasons.

Diplomacy and the Politics of National Reconciliation

Under Gorbachev a centerpiece of Soviet strategy in the Third World has been public calls for governments of national reconciliation. Until 1988 the Soviets usually specified terms in southern Africa that made reconciliation difficult, given the circumstances in the region. The basic idea was to appear conciliatory, but increase the military pressure to improve Moscow's leverage in any talks. For example, the USSR consistently supported a government of national reconciliation in Angola, subject to two major conditions. First, Jonas Savimbi, the charismatic leader of UNITA, was to be excluded from any government of national reconciliation. Second, South Africa was to withdraw from Angola and Namibia before the Cubans withdrew from Angola. As such, the Soviet position bore the mark of a public relations ploy, a hallmark of Gorbachev's foreign policy.

However, the Soviet stance was more sophisticated than might appear at first glance because it included an implicit fallback position. Should UNITA and South Africa accept Moscow's proposals, then the USSR would be in a position to portray itself as, in effect, the liberator of Namibia and the successful defender of Angola.

In the 1988 negotiations among Cuba, Angola, and South Africa, the USSR participated as an observer, thus maintaining its public diplomacy stance that it would not negotiate with South Africa. In fact, the Soviet observer, Vladilen I. Vasev, the head of the Southern Africa Department of the Soviet Foreign Ministry, was holding a series of secret meetings with the South African director general of foreign affairs, Neil van Heerden.[6]

In December 1988 the first widely known meeting in four decades took place between high-level Soviet and South African officials at the talks in Brazzaville over a tentative protocol on verification of the Cuban and South African withdrawals from Angola and Namibia, respectively. Soviet deputy foreign minister Anatoly L. Adamishin met with South African foreign minister Pik Botha, who then abruptly left the talks with his entire delegation in tow, an action that suggested verification remained a serious obstacle to implementing the withdrawals.[7] In Mexico City, Fidel Castro asserted that verification was none of South Africa's business and threatened to stay in Angola for ten more years. But a tentative protocol and final agreement were signed in late December.[8]

Privately, the USSR had indicated that once its clients reached an agreement, it would be willing to weigh in as a guarantor. The USSR sought a position with the United States on a proposed joint monitoring commission to verify the prospective withdrawals from Namibia and Angola. Such a joint commission would insert Soviet personnel into Namibia, from which they had heretofore been totally excluded.[9] The appearance of parity with the United States in resolving regional conflicts had been a major Soviet foreign policy objective for some time.[10]

As guarantor and joint monitor the Kremlin would then have saved face, a major concern for Moscow in the long Angolan civil war. In addition, the USSR would have positioned itself for an extended effort to enhance the influence of SWAPO in Namibia while tightening its grip on this occasionally recalcitrant client. Eventually, Namibia might provide another springboard for ANC efforts to influence the struggle inside South Africa. Of course, the success of SWAPO with Soviet backing would greatly encourage the ANC and probably increase Soviet influence in it.

The Soviet public diplomacy position anticipated either a South African withdrawal from Namibia or a permanent presence in southwestern Africa. In fact, the USSR only partially achieved its objective. The 1988 accords invited the USSR and the United States to serve as observers on the commission to monitor the peace process. Thus, Moscow appeared as a coequal but without the powers of a guarantor.

After consistently blocking U.S. mediation efforts, the apparent willingness of the USSR to work with the United States for a diplomatic solution to the Angolan and Namibian problems in 1988 represented in part a tactical response to the Reagan Doctrine, which advocated aid to opponents of radical socialist regimes with close Soviet ties. It also reflected Moscow's growing concern for the financial costs. As Yevgeny A. Tarabin, a senior analyst at the Africa Institute, put it,

> We are not going to go on spending money on armed forces for nothing. Angola has cost us billions. The United States has spent only some $30 million in aid there to UNITA, while we have spent 10 to 20 times more than that. What for? We need money for other purposes.[11]

The Soviets had come to view their escalating involvement in southwestern Africa as too expensive politically as well as economically, especially in the context of *perestroika*. The U.S. aid to the Angolan insurgents, the prospect of escalating South African military involvement, the U.S. linkage of regional conflict resolution to other areas of importance to Moscow, and the concern for renewal at home rendered the Kremlin more amenable to a political settlement in southwestern Africa.

Let us turn now to an examination of some of the instruments of Soviet coercive diplomacy—gunboat diplomacy and proxies.

Power Projection Through Gunboat Diplomacy

Soviet naval activities in southern Africa reflect a significant escalation of the Soviet Union's capacity to employ naval power to protect its interests in the region. There is not yet a full-fledged base there, but the gradual expansion and diversification of support facilities may not require such a politically provocative move. At present, Moscow is unlikely to go beyond defending its clients, but its capability to do so in a carefully calibrated fashion is being augmented, however slowly, and should not be regarded lightly.

The politico-military mission of the Soviet navy has been much underestimated.[12] Employing Soviet naval power to enhance its leverage in nonwar situations has proved surprisingly successful in the southern African region, which suggests an increasing willingness on the Soviet Union's part to employ higher levels of naval pressure there.

In 1981 both Mozambique and Angola received floating Soviet dry docks, reflecting the slow, incremental development of diversified strategic facilities designed to service the Soviet fleet.[13] This fleet has been deployed several times in an almost classic gunboat diplomacy fashion in support of Soviet clients in the region.

In 1976 the fleet fired on forces attacking the MPLA; in 1978 it fired on Ethiopian rebels;[14] and in 1981 it threatened to fire on the South Africans if they continued to raid ANC sanctuaries in Mozambique. This task force, which appeared in the harbor of Mozambique's capital, included the 16,000-ton carrier *Alexander Suvorov*.[15] In 1983 a Soviet task force again appeared in Maputo harbor to warn South Africa when Mozambique insurgents threatened that capital city. The missile age makes it increasingly possible to hit South African targets with sea-launched missiles, and although doing so would be extraordinarily provocative, the deterrent effect of such a capability is significant. The Kremlin's ability to deploy naval firepower capable of long-distance bombardment was underlined by the appearance in 1980 of one of its new class of cruisers that carry missiles with a range of 250 miles. Another new class of cruisers has the ability to protect these bombardment cruisers from air attack.[16]

There are three major reasons for the Soviet naval presence, other than supporting its clients. The first is to protect Soviet fishing vessels that ply the African littoral from east to west. African fish supply a large proportion of Soviet protein needs, and the USSR has fishing treaties with most of these states. Soviet methods have provoked severe criticism, for Moscow literally vacuums the waters, depleting them enough to warrant public outbursts in Angola, Mozambique, Namibia, and South Africa, which have extended coastlines.

Second, there is some concern about the presence of U.S. strategic submarines in the Indian Ocean. Third, the Soviet naval presence reminds the West that its oil and mineral supplies could be cut off in wartime. Even in peacetime such an act would be an act of war, but Soviet harassment of the cape oil and mineral route at some level below that of anticipated U.S. involvement is probable under certain circumstances. The experience of the fleet over the past decade and the expanded network of facilities render such an exercise more possible.

As Richard Bissell points out, it is often forgotten that in the Angolan crisis of 1975 the USSR deployed the nucleus of an anticarrier warfare group in the South Atlantic that effectively deterred the United States from sending a task force under the carrier USS *Enterprise* to these waters.[17] During the crisis, Moscow dispatched to the area a cruiser and a destroyer, both armed with guided missiles.[18] The Soviet task force also included an amphibious landing ship with naval infantry on board and several other auxiliaries. Some evidence indicates that three other missile-armed ships may have been kept in reserve near the Strait of Gibraltar. Before its intervention the USSR had concluded thirteen agreements for access to ports along the African coast.

The Soviet force first tried to neutralize Zairian patrol boats against the large quantities of Soviet equipment arriving for the MPLA by sea. Subsequent maneuvers indicated preparations for withdrawing Soviet advisers when the tide temporarily turned against the MPLA before the massive airlift of Cuban troops.

Soviet sensitivity to the public diplomacy repercussions of such dramatic and heretofore unprecedented activities is reflected in the withdrawal of the *Kresta II* SSM cruiser and the Kotlin-class guided missile destroyer during the OAU summit meeting on the Angolan crisis in January 1976.

More recently, in December 1983, the USSR sent the largest task force to round the Cape of Good Hope since 1979 to back up its warning to South Africa about invading Angola (Operation Askari). It included an aircraft carrier and three surface vessels, and it stopped in the Angolan capital to underline Moscow's commitment to its client. The 1979 flotilla had included the aircraft carrier *Kiev*. In August 1981 a Soviet task force stood off the Cunene River in Angola to threaten South African forces raiding SWAPO sanctuaries there. At one time or another the USSR has had between 15 and 35 warships and auxiliaries in the southern African region. In short, the

USSR has demonstrated considerable flexibility in the use of its navy in the region.

Power Projection and Coercive Diplomacy: The Proxy Technique

As Adam Ulam has pointed out the insertion of a large proxy army into Angola in 1975–1976 represented a new technique of Soviet foreign policy.[19] Militarily, the Afghan intervention was fundamentally different. Because Soviet combat units were involved, they could be immediately resupplied because of Afghanistan's location adjacent to the USSR. The proxy technique is particularly valuable for power projection far from the Soviet periphery, where the use of combat units from the USSR would be excessively provocative to the United States.

The proxy technique enables Moscow to use force, while avoiding war, by carefully employing the force of others at levels below that of anticipated U.S. involvement. It is low-intensity warfare by proxy.

As Fidel Castro proclaimed to ambassadors from the nonaligned states in May 1988 after inserting ten thousand new troops in Angola, "We don't want a military victory over South Africa; we want a global negotiated political solution. But now the balance of forces favors us."[20]

As this author put it in 1976,

> Soviet activities in Angola bear the mark of a relatively restrained, carefully orchestrated test of American intentions and will in the post-Vietnam era, as well as experimentation with an essentially new mode of expanding its influence—proxy war. What is notable is the complexity of the operation, the congeries of instruments employed, and the modulated deployment of these instruments. There was little disproportion between the means and the ends. Simultaneously, the USSR appears acutely sensitive to the highly symbolic impact of employing military force, however minimal, on the perceptions of political leaders throughout the globe.[21]

For these reasons and others, it is worth recounting some of the chief proxy tactics employed by the surrogates of the USSR in the specific setting of southern Africa. It is also important to identify the political advantages and disadvantages of employing surrogates like Cuba and East Germany, as demonstrated by specific episodes and instances in the region over the past two decades.

The Cuban Proxy: An Army, Not Advisers. First, the most important aspect of the proxy technique in southern Africa is the presence of a proxy army. Up to 56,000 Cubans were in Angola.[22] This was an army that was keeping a small urban elite and ethnic minority in power. The Cubans are active elsewhere in Africa and Latin America, but in southern Africa they had been fighting off and on as an army since 1975. They were not just advisers and trainers.

The Proxy Technique: Joint Operations with Soviets. A second important aspect of the proxy technique is joint combined operations by the proxies. The presence of large numbers of Soviet advisers down to the battalion level with the Angolan army almost amounted to joint military operations.[23] The Soviets denied that there were combat troops in Angola, but with so many advisers in each battalion, the USSR had come as close to a formal commitment of troops as possible while still avoiding this politically provocative act.[24] This is a good example of how carefully Moscow finetunes and orchestrates its politico-military strategy.

The Proxy Technique: Joint Operations with Cubans. A second example of joint operations is the combined SWAPO-Cuban units, which appeared in southern Angola in 1988. Here Cuba was protecting SWAPO, training it on-the-job and facilitating its incursions into Namibia by retarding South African raids on its sanctuaries while enabling SWAPO to get close to Namibia. South Africa's counterinsurgency strategy had been to hit guerrilla infiltration units deep in Angola before they could get to Namibia. Combined operations made this South African strategy much more risky while decreasing the risk for the SWAPO insurgents seeking to penetrate northern Namibia. Symbolically, this again avoids the more provocative act of deploying an identifiable foreign army.

The Proxy Technique: Soviet Air Defense. For most of this decade, the USSR has been pursuing a policy designed to gradually achieve air superiority in southern Angola and Namibia. Since 1981 the USSR has deployed increasingly sophisticated air defense systems in the form of advanced planes, radar, and missiles manned by Soviets and East Germans. The major South African raid into Angola in 1981 (Operation Protea), in which Russians were killed and captured, was aimed primarily at new missile and radar systems. For the first time the SAM-6 missile had appeared outside the Warsaw Pact.

Air superiority was a key to stopping SWAPO and to protecting UNITA. The South Africans have limited and somewhat antiquated planes, although they are working on the Cheetah, which reportedly would be able to match the Soviet planes now in the region. The South African pilots are superb, but the Soviets and Cubans and reportedly even some East Germans have been good also. The Angolans were improving under the guidance of Soviet advisers at Lubango in southern Angola.

It became increasingly dangerous for South African pilots to attack the radar network along the string of Soviet-built bases in southern Angola. They relied on UNITA spies telling them when the radar was turned off before attacking. This neutralized the Soviet missiles, but not necessarily the Soviet planes.

For example, the MIG-29, which Zimbabwe considered buying, is potentially superior to anything South Africa possesses. The USSR has slowly improved the air capability of its Angolan client and attempted to do so with Zimbabwe, all of which tends to enhance its influence. However, the USSR has not introduced the most advanced equipment to avoid dramatic provocations, demonstrating an acute sensitivity to the risks of major escalations, preferring to slowly calibrate its involvement upward over an extended period. At the height of the Angola-Namibia peace talks in the summer of 1988, the Soviets and their clients virtually achieved air superiority in southern Angola, which provided a major impetus for South Africa to compromise.

The Proxy Technique: Specialized Functions. During the 1988 siege of Cuito Cuanavale, the key Angolan air base in the south, North Vietnamese advisers arrived in the capital, Luanda. Apparently their function was to advise on how to resist siege tactics, based on Vietnamese experience with the French at Dien Bien Phu in the 1950s. This is just one example of the specialized functions delegated to a congeries of proxies from around the world.

At various times, the East Germans have handled communication and radar in Angola and Mozambique. They trained the security and intelligence personnel in both Afro-Marxist states. They also trained SWAPO and the ANC in insurgency and sabotage tactics and techniques. For a while, the East Germans were delegated the responsibility for planning and administering Soviet strategy in the area, but after their poor performance during the Zimbabwean insurgency, this was apparently rescinded.

Of course, the Soviets have manned tanks and artillery in combat, and the Cubans have served first as combat troops, then primarily on garrison duty, and in 1988 again as combat troops and in joint units with SWAPO insurgents.

At one time there was speculation that Soviet units were sent to Cuba to relieve Cuban troops for duty in Angola. This raises the question of whether special Soviet units might be deployed in southern Africa to relieve other proxies for combat.

Most analysts agree that a massive rapid deployment like that in Ethiopia would be too risky in this region for several reasons. First, the distance is enormous. Second, the South African forces are much more effective than the Somalis. Finally, the exercise might provoke U.S. intervention and a serious escalation. However, here again the deployment of ten thousand to twelve thousand crack Cuban troops in a few months in the spring of 1988 comes very close to a rapid deployment exercise, though the use of a proxy is less provocative and, of course, deniable. Also, the discreet deployment of experienced special units from Afghanistan to relieve other proxy forces for combat is possible under certain circumstances. This would fit the basic pattern of gradual escalation of Soviet-proxy involvement for over a decade.

In mid-1988 reliable evidence of Soviet use of chemical warfare amidst a major escalation of the conflict in Angola indicated that some Afghan tactics might be used.[25] Some Angolan officers have received instruction in aspects of chemical warfare.[26] The willingness of Moscow to employ force in the region has been consistently underestimated. A dramatic example of Soviet aggressiveness occurred when the Kremlin attempted a last-minute salvage of its ultimately unsuccessful client during the Zimbabwe uprising, an episode worth recounting.[27]

In 1979 the USSR proposed a complex initiative that raised the prospect of a major conflict involving the entire spectrum of Soviet proxies. Its immediate purpose was twofold: to retard Mugabe's influence among the insurgents and to forestall Western recognition of the government of Bishop Abel Muzorewa. Although neither purpose was achieved, in the process the Soviets revealed a willingness to take unusual risks in southern Africa as a major insurgency drew to a close. Because there were four major insurgencies in the region in 1988, this is particularly relevant.

The Soviet plan went as follows. A high Cuban official proposed to some frontline state leaders that the Soviets' client, Joshua Nkomo, and Mugabe, whose troops had done most of the fighting, meet inside Zimbabwe (formerly Rhodesia) not far from the South African border under the protection of Mozambique's regular army to declare themselves the legal government. The presidents of Angola and Ethiopia were also involved. The East Germans promised massive military assistance. Thus the entire spectrum of Soviet proxies was to be included in a venture that might have provoked an extraordinary South African reaction.

Because the Cubans claimed to speak for the entire "socialist community," it appears that the USSR was prepared to risk a major escalation—if not to a conventional war, then to a quasi war. However, the Soviets proved inept in rallying their clients. Nkomo himself opposed the plan, and the Ethiopians ultimately backed off, which led to Angola's reneging and Mozambique's holding the bag.

Nevertheless, it is significant that the USSR and its proxies accepted the risks of a major confrontation with the powerful Republic of South Africa, even though military strategists might argue that their logistic support and infrastructure were inadequate to the task of honoring their commitments. Soviet military ingenuity should not be underestimated, especially in Africa, where the Soviets have proved unusually innovative.

The Proxy Technique: Assets and Liabilities. There are positive and negative aspects of using proxy forces, as illustrated repeatedly in southern Africa. Some are obvious, others more subtle. The Cubans adapted to Angola more easily and were more acceptable than the East Germans or the Soviets for cultural and ethnic reasons. Because the Cubans spoke Spanish, their ability to communicate in Portuguese was greater. Also, most of the first Cubans to arrive were black, and, in fact, many were descendants of Angolan slaves. Liberating the descendants of their ancestors was a major theme of Cuban propaganda and public diplomacy.

Perhaps the major advantage of using proxies, other than the obvious one—that Soviet casualties are minimized—is deniability. In other words, the USSR can disassociate itself from the acts of the proxy. This helps avoid confrontations with the United States and even with South Africa, thus retarding major escalations that could threaten Soviet prestige. For example, the USSR claimed that Cuba suggested the initial 1975 intervention in Angola, and in 1988 the Soviets benefited from the perception that Castro was more militant in southern Africa than Moscow.

In the summer of 1988, Cuba, not the Soviet Union, negotiated with South Africa, so the Kremlin can claim that it has been only marginally involved and has refused to negotiate with that "pariah." Finally, if the Cubans are defeated militarily or withdraw, the implications are not nearly so serious for Moscow's global image.

Perhaps the most dramatic example of the advantages of deniability relates to Zimbabwe, where the East Germans were responsible for orchestrating Soviet support for the insurgency. The East Germans bungled the operation, but the USSR hid behind the proxy veil, thus expediting the development of normal relations after independence when Robert Mugabe, who was not the Soviet candidate-client, came to power.

Shortly before Mugabe's victory, the East Germans told several leaders of his party (ZANU) that they regarded it as a "splinter group." At approximately the same time, before discussing aid, the East Germans attempted to persuade ZANU to sign a document denouncing the Chinese invasion of Vietnam. Until then China had been ZANU's chief source of arms. This kind of episode highlights the negative and positive sides of employing a proxy. It was a monumental miscalculation, but it was at least partially deniable that it represented Soviet policy.

However, the USSR could never be entirely clean in the eyes of Mugabe and his party. The Soviets had refused a meeting in Moscow with the entire ZANU Central Committee, a meeting arranged by the president of Tanzania, Julius Nyerere, as the insurgency reached its climax. The Russians also demonstrated their ineptness in handling ZANU when, in return for a few arms, they demanded a written statement from Mugabe recognizing his rival, Nkomo, as leader of the insurgents. Nevertheless, the alleged East German responsibility for supporting Nkomo provided for both Gorbachev and Mugabe a fig leaf that facilitated the resumption of normal diplomatic relations between the USSR and Zimbabwe, and the incident was shuffled under the table.

The chief disadvantage of using a proxy is that at times the tail must wag the dog. For example, the flamboyant Castro is certainly motivated by the prospect of being perceived around the world as the "liberator" of southern Africa, which partially accounts for his statements about not leaving southern Africa until "apartheid falls."[28] Some evidence suggests the USSR has instructed him to abandon this theme, but to little avail. There is also evidence that the USSR was displeased by the use of Cuban troops in 1987 to quell a rebellion inside the MPLA against President Neto, who was not a Soviet favorite.

Castro's statements that Cuba will stay in Africa until apartheid is overthrown may have troubled the USSR while Cuba and South Africa were negotiating in the summer of 1988, but this should not be construed as a fundamental policy difference. Castro was, of course, seeking the limelight as always, but too much has been made over the years of these supposed differences. Castro openly criticized the USSR for its Angolan tactics in a speech in late July 1988, but he went on to say that relations between his country and the USSR had never been better.[29] In fact, the long-range strategies of the two communist states are almost identical, as the following passage from a lecture by the Soviet second deputy foreign minister for African affairs, then ambassador to Lesotho, illustrates:

> For 15 years the [southern African] region has continued to be the zone of one of the bloodiest and most protracted conflicts in modern history. In the past decade it has become a real threat to international stability. The main cause of this conflict is the system of apartheid. *Unless this system is abolished the rules of the conflict will stay intact* [emphasis added].[30]

Another example of at least the potential for the proxy exceeding the wishes of its patron is Eastern Europe's great concern for access to minerals, which, as Christopher Coker pointed out, has led to militant statements bordering on threats of military action by some East European commentators.[31]

The last major disadvantage of employing a proxy is that its incompetence may undermine the patron's strategy. In the late 1970s the East Germans seemed most inept in Zimbabwe and Mozambique, and Cuban troops performed miserably until the late 1980s in Angola. However, despite these disadvantages, there is no substitute for an army and advisers who will take casualties that further the patron's aims.

Friction Between Patron and Client

Moscow has found that manipulating dynamic and often charismatic leaders of insurgencies and newly independent states in southern Africa is no easy task. Examples of conflict between patron and client abound. The Kremlin never trusted Augustino Neto, the poet and physician who emerged as the first president of Angola, and the feeling was mutual. As Vasily Kuznetsov, a high-ranking Soviet diplomat, put it, "Psychologically he's not all that reliable." [32] For his part, Neto declared publicly at the height of the civil war that "Angola will never be enslaved to any foreign country, be it the USSR or any other power. Never!" [33] The Soviets withdrew support from Neto in favor of Daniel Chipenda from 1973 to 1974, only restoring it (admittedly in a massive fashion) in 1975, just before Neto's victory.

The Soviet's preferred candidate for the leadership, Iko Carreira, eventually, even after spending three years in the USSR, emerged as an advocate of buying weapons from the West. For taking this position he was removed from his high military post and, in effect, exiled to Algeria as ambassador.[34] In 1988, President dos Santos, once married to a Russian, was reportedly furious at the USSR for pressuring him to settle with UNITA.

On November 11, 1987, in a 30-minute Soviet television show, a Russian correspondent, in unusually graphic terms, criticized Angola's government. Among other things he asserted that "the middle rung of the state apparatus is openly hindering the decisions of the party. Corruption is at an unprecedented level and inflation is rampant. One thing is clear. Angola's present situation cannot continue for long." [35]

In short, Soviet-MPLA friction has a long history and is continuing. Also, some reports indicate that the Angolan army deeply resents the superior food and housing provided the Cubans,[36] a kind of friction that has surfaced in other episodes in the region. For example, during the insurgency in Zimbabwe, the Kremlin not only opposed the successful rebel, Robert Mugabe, but was unable to control its own client, Joshua Nkomo, at the critical moment. The Soviets and Cubans devised a plan to set up a liberated zone for Nkomo, but he refused to cooperate and negotiated with the West, contrary to Soviet instructions.[37]

As noted in detail in chapter 3, there is a long history of friction between the ANC and Moscow. In the mid-1980s this revolved around the use of violence. The young radicals pressed for dramatic escalation, but the SACP, the Kremlin's chief instrument inside the ANC, cautioned against premature acts of violence that precipitate a counterproductive reaction before appropriate political preparations have been made. In short, Moscow preferred stressing political stratagems, and the ANC radicals preferred more violence.

Friction between patron and client in the Namibian rebellion has been more sporadic. The KGB found the Namibians' revolutionary readiness appalling, but it underestimated their indigenous support (see chapters 1 and 3). The release from his South African prison of Herman Toivo, a prominent founder of SWAPO who has few ties to the Soviets, rendered SWAPO somewhat less malleable. Some top SWAPO leaders have even publicly expressed a preference for a mixed economy rather than an Afro-Marxist one like that in Angola and Mozambique.

The Soviet military has such a low opinion of the insurgents, SWAPO and the ANC, that according to one source they "miss no opportunity" to point out how low "national liberation" is on the Soviets' priority list. This can hardly endear them to their clients.[38]

Despite these difficulties, the USSR has demonstrated considerable resilience and persistence. As the previous chapters illustrate, Moscow has reacted to each setback, whether in Zaire or Zimbabwe or in relations with its Afro-Marxist clients and the insurgents, by reassessing its tactics and pressing forward with new stratagems.

Exploiting the chronic instability in southern Africa to enhance Moscow's influence worldwide, as well as in the region, has been a central objective of Soviet policy in the area since Krushchev.[39] Whenever costs and risks escalate, the Kremlin backs off and attempts to consolidate its gains while resorting to more innovative diplomatic initiatives in arenas like the nonaligned states. There is nothing new in this fundamental strategic approach. Lenin employed it at Brest Litovsk to deal with his most immediate foreign policy problem and in the New Economic Policy to deal with his most pressing economic problems.

Although the Brezhnev regime proved to be extraordinarily innovative in its tactical adaptation of proxy war in southern Africa, Andropov and Chernenko encouraged a steady expansion of Soviet involvement with the nonaligned states. Gorbachev and his new team are fine-tuning what went before, especially in the public diplomacy arena.

Soviet behavior indicates that Gorbachev's policy in this region may be conditioned more by the economic costs than was the case in previous regimes; but this is far from certain because, although there is an effort to minimize the costs in Mozambique, the commitment to Angola reached an all-time high in 1988. What emerges from the pattern of Soviet behavior is a more sophisticated and carefully calibrated balancing of military, economic, and diplomatic initiatives designed to maximize Soviet influence throughout the region at the least cost and risk.

9

SOVIET STRATEGY

Motivations, Perceptions, Continuity

Assessing Soviet motivations and intentions is admittedly an imprecise exercise, but because the USSR has been massively involved in southern Africa since 1975 its activities do provide some basis on which to make a judgment. The Soviet Union's behavior over this period suggests two major motivations for its involvement: access to strategic facilities (naval and air) and minerals, particularly for its allies in Eastern Europe, and the public diplomacy objective of portraying the USSR as the bulwark of "progressive" forces and as a global superpower capable of intervening anywhere in the world.

Access to Naval and Air Facilities: A Steadily Enhanced Presence

Moscow has been somewhat frustrated in its efforts to acquire permanent bases in southern Africa; however, it has slowly and steadily increased its access to naval and air facilities.[1] Since 1977 Soviet combatant and noncombatant ships have paid regular visits to the Mozambican ports of Ncala, Maputo, and Beira, and in 1981 the USSR installed a dry dock. But Mozambique has refused the USSR permission to construct a permanent base.

In Angola the USSR has succeeded in acquiring access to what amounts to three minibases: in Luanda, the capital; Lobito, the largest harbor; and Namibe, on the south coast.

From Luanda the USSR flies reconnaissance covering most of the Atlantic. These maritime surveillance missions are carried out by the TU-95 Bear reconnaissance aircraft once stationed in Conakry, Guinea, but transferred to Luanda after Guinea revoked Soviet rights in a 1981 dispute. Luanda provides a natural, sheltered tidal harbor with depths of up to 100 feet. Although there are no major shipyards or repair installations, the foundry does perform minor above-water repairs. In 1981 the USSR installed a dry dock.

Lobito, the largest port, has a natural coastal harbor protected by a peninsula with deep-water facilities capable of repairing major damage to ships. Namibe on the arid southern coast provides anchorages at depths of up to 56 feet and good breathing space at its main pier. The Soviets have steadily improved the port because it supplies SWAPO and the forces deployed against Savimbi.

Access to facilities and transit rights in Benin, Mali, the Congo, Guinea, Mali, and Cape Verde, as well as in Ethiopia at the Asmara airfield and dry dock and bunkering facilities at Dahlak Island, represent a significant military advantage. At various times, they have served to reinforce Moscow's capability to lift supplies and personnel by air and sea to southern Africa. During the Cuban intervention, planes flew through Barbados to Angola (as many as fifteen flights per day) and later from Cuba (Holguin) to the Congo. An air route through Mali offers a potentially shorter alternative to the old route through Guinea. In Cape Verde, Sal Island is used as a way station for Cubans and Soviets going to southern Africa.

In summary, the USSR has been building a network of air and naval facilities that provide it with a variety of opportunities to expand its influence in the region without the expense of maintaining major bases. The cost and risk of losing such facilities are far less than for a base. As the Soviets learned from their Conakry experience, access to facilities can be quickly and inexpensively replaced and facilities do not provoke local resentment as easily or attract superpower attention as dramatically. Moscow's past behavior suggests it will continue to focus on enhancing its access to naval and air facilities, as indicated by its pressure on South Africa to give up Walvis Bay in Namibia.

Soviet Interests in Strategic Minerals

As Lewis Gann and Peter Duignan pointed out in 1981, a major Soviet strategic interest in southern Africa has always been that region's strategic minerals (see table 12).[2] For years the USSR sold manganese, platinum, and chromite to the West, but this changed at the beginning of the 1980s with exports of these minerals dropping 50 percent or more. Moscow even began to import these minerals.[3] This suggests that access to these minerals may be an increasingly important motivation of Soviet foreign policy for southern Africa.[4] In the spring of 1989, when Soviet deputy foreign minister Anatoly Adamishin was in South Africa as an official observer on the Angola/Namibia peace commission, he took a three-hour helicopter tour of Witwatersrand, the heart of the South African mining industry.

Also new is the increasing interest of the East European states in the region's minerals, as Christopher Coker has dramatically demonstrated.[5] Of the two-hundred Council for Mutual Economic Assistance enterprises in the Third World, half are in Africa; 75 percent of them are in southern Africa, mostly in mining.[6] Coker argues that Eastern Europe is increasingly concerned both about protecting its investments in mining in the area and about its future access to minerals. Coker tends to confirm the insights of Duignan and Gann: that as Soviet mineral reserves diminish and become more expensive to extract, Moscow's interest in access to southern Africa's minerals may grow.

Southern Africa's vast mineral resources have been a factor in international relations since their discovery in the late nineteenth century, and there is no doubt that the Soviets are interested in them. However, there is little indication that the Kremlin is willing to take unusual risks to ensure access to them. Because it is generally accepted that the minerals in South Africa and Namibia are important to U.S. national security, it is highly probable that the United States would respond dramatically to any overt attempt to deny U.S. access. Although the Soviets are not prepared to accept a risk of this magnitude, they have demonstrated a willingness to turn a quick profit by acquiring minerals when extraordinary opportunities present themselves. If the Soviet strategic presence in the region continues to grow, its approach to the question of strategic minerals could change.

Because the USSR possesses most of the same minerals as southern Africa, an important short-term interest, as in any large corporation, is in orderly markets. Seeking reliable profits for foreign sales based on an orderly international pricing mechanism, the Soviets have established an elaborate institutional structure to market their minerals, especially gold. There are Soviet-owned banks in every major money market in the world except New

TABLE 12
PERCENT OF WORLD RESERVES OF STRATEGIC MINERALS IN ANGOLA, MOZAMBIQUE, AND SOUTH AFRICA

Platinum	94%
Gold	72%
Vanadium	70%
Chromium	67%
Manganese	62%
Asbestos	47%
Uranium	43%
Fluorspar	26%

SOURCE: W. C. J. van Rensburg and D. A. Pretorius, *South Africa's Strategic Minerals* (FAA Publication Series, 1977).

York, and the Soviet banks in London, Zurich, Frankfurt, and Singapore are quite sophisticated.[7]

There is growing evidence that the Soviets have established somewhat regular, if indirect, contacts with mineral brokers in southern Africa, particularly in the gold, platinum, and diamond fields. Kurt Campbell has produced substantial evidence of Soviet cooperation with South African corporations to stabilize mineral prices.[8] One South African company has marketed Soviet diamonds for years,[9] and specialized Soviet research centers such as Kiev's Institute of Superhard Metals consult with South African experts.

The South Africans have the same interest in orderly markets as the Soviets. There is nothing especially unusual about this from the Soviets' point of view; for them, it is business as usual. One of the largest Soviet projects in Africa is a joint venture with Morocco for refining phosphate. At the same time, the USSR helps arm the Polisario insurgents, who are fighting a major guerrilla war against Morocco. Similarly, the Soviets are the major supporters of the ANC, which is conducting a campaign of sabotage and subversion inside the Republic of South Africa.

Throughout its history the USSR has conducted its foreign policy on two levels: traditional political and economic contacts and covert activities. Although it has no diplomatic relations or overt trade with South Africa, informal contacts with its business interests are likely where it benefits both parties, despite the apparent contradiction of supporting the forces attempting to overthrow the regime.

Soviet cooperation with the southern African minerals industry does not amount to a cartel. Essentially, the free market system is permitted to operate so that prices fluctuate in an orderly fashion, except when the USSR takes advantage of an extraordinary political circumstance that offers an opportunity for quick profit taking.

During the Rhodesian conflict, the Kremlin bought chrome, in violation of U.N. sanctions, from Rhodesia and sold it at the inflated prices resulting from those sanctions. Even more dramatically, the Soviets planes flew to Shaba in southern Zaire to carry away huge quantities of cobalt just before the invasion of that country from neighboring Marxist Angola.[10] The cobalt was later sold at the inflated prices resulting from the shutdown of mining operations caused by the invasion. Although Soviet propaganda seeks to discredit Western imperialists for exploiting the mineral resources and people in southern Africa, the guiding principle of its own policy there has been guaranteed profit maximization.

The USSR has demonstrated considerable ingenuity as an entrepreneur with respect to the minerals in southern Africa, again earning a profit for the Soviet state. In the short run, the USSR does not seek to *control* the minerals of southern Africa in order to *deny* them to the West, at least in the foreseeable future, for this would be a virtual act of war. Most Soviet behavior reflects a policy carefully designed to maximize its political and economic influence short of war, but the episodes in Rhodesia and Shaba reflect experience with a kind of quasi cartel.

The Soviets can be expected to take advantage of this kind of market disruption when it occurs and even at times to facilitate such disruption. Despite the claims of some analysts that avoiding disruption of mining in South Africa is a guiding principle of Soviet policy in the area, Moscow's previous behavior suggests that it can extract some benefit from such events. After all, because the USSR possesses many of the same minerals, a cutoff or diminution of South African supplies would dramatically enhance the value of Soviet reserves.

Determining whether the USSR or its Eastern European clients would resort to force to maintain or deny access remains a highly speculative exercise. The growing network of air and naval facilities makes this more probable and possible, but in the early 1980s East German technicians had to stand by helplessly while Mozambican rebels attacked the coal mines where they were working.

It is highly probable that the price of these minerals would be raised if more pro-Soviet regimes emerge throughout the region. The Soviet experience with quasi cartels during the Rhodesian and Shaba crises provides evidence for this. What is certain is that the Eastern bloc's increasing dependence on southern Africa's minerals suggests a continuing high level of involvement with the region.

Soviet Perceptions of Africa

Soviet understanding of African realities has evolved slowly, especially among decision makers, despite Moscow's steadily escalating involvement and a plethora of academic advice. A major reason for this is Soviet ideology, with its orientation toward class struggle, which makes it hard for the Soviets to appreciate the intensity of ethnic ties in Africa. In Angola the UNITA insurgency, opposed by the USSR since 1974, draws most of its support from the Ovimbundu tribe, the largest in the country. In South Africa the chief black opposition to Moscow's client, the ANC, is Inkatha, a political organization based primarily on the Zulu tribe, the largest and most powerful in that country. The Kremlin opposed the insurgent movement in Zimbabwe that was backed by the Shona-speaking tribes, which is far and away the predominant ethnic group.

From the multifarious academic analyses of Africa by Soviet specialists, an awareness of the importance of ethnic bonds seems to be emerging, but there is no clear consensus.[11] The Soviet experts on Africa refer to the ethnic factor as the problem of "special characteristics."[12] Although some specialists recognize the problem, few fully appreciate how profoundly it affects regional politics. So the endless debates among Soviet Africanists on the course of development in Africa probably yield less guidance to the decision makers than is generally assumed, which suggests that further setbacks based on faulty analysis and understanding of the basic political realities in Africa can be expected. Because Alexander N. Yakovlev, Gorbachev's chief foreign policy adviser, and all the deputy foreign ministers for the Third World are globalists, these regional realities may be slighted even further.

There is some evidence that Gorbachev himself tends to view ethnicity in terms of Soviet central Asia. In a conversation with Congressman Mickey Leland, he suggested that ethnic problems in America might be solved by employing the Soviet central Asian model.[13] In other words, ethnic groups should be assigned to separate geographic entities. This suggests that the general secretary's image of Africa is influenced by the Soviet experience with the Muslims of central Asia.[14] Gorbachev, whose early career in the party involved mass resettlement of Muslims deported by Stalin during World War II, in fact grew up in an area with a large Muslim population.[15]

During the period when Gorbachev was climbing to the top of the party apparatus, the Muslim republics were regarded as "an important asset in the promotion of Soviet foreign policy objectives in the Third World because they serve as an example of how backward societies can successfully build socialism, while bypassing the capitalist stage of development."[16]

As Petr Manchka, a deputy director of the CPSU International Department and head of its African section in the 1970s, put it, the countries of socialist orientation "are approximately at the beginning of a path similar to that which the peoples of the Khorezm and Bukhara People's Soviet Republic took. As is well known, Khorezm and Bukhara [in Soviet central Asia] in a comparatively short time—the period of one generation—moved from being patriarchal and medieval societies to socialism, bypassing the stage of capitalism."[17]

As long ago as 1975, Manchka pointed out the obvious differences between central Asia and socialist-oriented Third World states, differences that constrain Soviet influence. The Third World states are enmeshed in the capitalist international economic system and can never expect such massive aid as central Asia, which is after all part of the USSR. These constraints have been often cited for the proposition that the central Asian model no longer conditions Soviet thinking, but in 1986 a dramatic example of the durability of this image surfaced.

Gleb Starushenko, the deputy director of the Africa Institute whose 1986 presentation foreshadowed the Kremlin's new emphasis on political stratagems, is an expert on Soviet nationalities, not southern Africa. His speech reflected the multinational mind-set of important academicians and probably Gorbachev himself. A centerpiece of Starushenko's talk was a constitutional proposal for South Africa in which each of its four communities (black, white, Indian, and colored) would be represented as groups in the upper house of a future legislature.[18] This would in effect perpetuate the present system of classification on a group basis. In fact, when Starushenko delivered his talk, the parliament of South Africa already had three chambers for whites, Indians, and coloreds, but it excluded blacks. Starushenko is known to be used as a barometer by the Soviets. In this case the ANC roundly denounced the proposal, but it is clear the Soviets are not wedded to the ANC's vision of a nonracial unitary state and are inclined to something more like their own multinational system.

Although some recent Soviet analysis reflects a more pessimistic view of Africa's development prospects, the generalized image of the central Asian model is deeply imbedded in the Soviet psyche because of the historical experience with early African leaders in the independence struggle who sought to imitate the central Asian model. Kwame Nkrumah, the first president of Ghana, made plans to form a "West African Soviet Republic" and frequently cited the applicability of the Soviet multinational structure to Africa.[19]

The Soviet Republic of Uzbekistan in particular became a showcase for visiting Afro-Asian dignitaries who were lectured on the value of this model in resolving ethnic conflict and facilitating economic development. The message was adopt a Soviet-style political system and a pro-Soviet foreign policy. Gorbachev appears to be a little more flexible, but seems to retain the basic image of central Asia as his mental framework for dealing with southern Africa in particular. Soviet behavior in the region reflects this.

African Perceptions of the USSR

What is salient about the central Asian model for this sophisticated generation of young African leaders is the persistence of the indigenous Muslim culture and the heavy hand of Soviet imperialism. The image of Gorbachev resettling Muslims deported by Stalin and the riots in Kazakhstan and Azerbaijan hardly reassure them that either the Soviets or their model are worth emulating. Comments by Gorbachev like, "We are not a country like Tanganyika, and you can't treat us as if we were," reflect an innate disdain for Africa often evident in the behavior of Soviet personnel in Africa.[20] In the USSR itself racial incidents involving African students at Soviet universities and especially on Soviet streets are commonplace.[21]

For the ANC and SWAPO there is a special irony in Gorbachev's comments to Congressman Leland calling for ethnic segregation into discrete geographic units because that is precisely what the ANC and SWAPO are rebelling against. Similarly, the ANC was quick to denounce Gleb Starushenko's constitutional proposals as incorporating the core features of apartheid.[22] Such indiscretion certainly mitigates the impact of Soviet public diplomacy initiatives.

Africa's image of the USSR's policy in central Asia is that of a Russian imperial power dominating the indigenous peoples. This offends Africans' fierce sense of independence and aggravates their suspicion of Soviet motives. It is clear to them that the price of development in Soviet central Asia is Russianization, especially since the Gorbachev Politburo, unlike its predecessors, has no central Asian representative. It was Gorbachev's replacement of a Kazakh by a Russian as head of the Kazakh Communist Party that caused riots there.

This political disenchantment with the Soviet multicultural model of economic development is compounded by the failure of the Soviet economy itself and the virtual collapse of the socialist economies in Angola and Mozambique, which in turn aggravated the civil wars in these two countries. To some extent, the civil war in Mozambique was caused by a mindless pursuit of socialist economic strategy.

Nonetheless, the Soviet political model—the Leninist party, small, tightly knit, and highly centralized—continues to maintain its attraction as a device for retaining power and ameliorating ethnic conflict. However, even here some rethinking has surfaced. Mozambique in particular has toyed with decentralization, and in both Angola and Mozambique the government seems to be ever so slowly eclipsing the party as a center of power. In sum, there is considerable disillusionment with the Soviet model of development, especially in the economic realm.

Conclusion: Continuity and Change

As Thomas Henriksen points out, perhaps the most important motivation of Soviet policy in Africa is Russian national interest. Historically, the Russian czar was involved in Africa for many of the reasons that the USSR is today.[23] Above all, the Russian Empire sought to diminish the relative influence of its chief opponents, first the Ottoman Empire, then the British. To buttress its claims as a navel power and to help mitigate the influence of the Ottomans and the British, the czars sought naval facilities along the East African littoral much like the Soviets in Angola and Mozambique.[24] To harass the British in particular, the czar sent aid to the Afrikaner insurgents during the Boer War and plotted to stir up a rebellion of the blacks against the new British regime in the early twentieth century.[25] He even considered a Russian protectorate over South Africa.[26]

When pressures elsewhere required attention, the Russians backed away from involvement in Africa. The plot to instigate a black insurgency in South Africa took a back seat when the Russo-Japanese crisis began to escalate. Strategic retreat—"two steps forward, one step back"—when the correlation of forces is unfavorable is a well-known Leninist tactic, not unfamiliar in practice, at least, to the Russian Empire.

After pressing forward for a while, the Russians seek a *peredyschka*, a respite, a breathing space, the need for which is inherent in much of Gorbachev's foreign policy. In the interim, Moscow usually indulges in fine-tuned probing for advantage, while seeking, above all, to extract the maximum advantage from public diplomacy opportunities.

Before 1945 the massive Soviet propaganda campaign in Africa proved enormously successful, as Edward Wilson has demonstrated.[27] Agitational work among youth, women, and labor unions played a significant role in drawing them into the political process, instilled in African leaders an understanding of the communist system, and inclined them to look on the Soviets with favor. This is exactly the strategy advocated for South Africa by leading Soviet analysts today, as the ANC seeks to consolidate its position, particularly in the unions and among the youth.

A decade of massive Soviet involvement and behavior indicates that the USSR will continue to defend Angola, press for Namibian independence and for bases in Mozambique—including Walvis Bay, and expand its more traditional presence in the nonaligned states while seeking greater access to minerals and strategic facilities and portraying itself around the world as the bulwark of so-called progressive forces like the ANC.

Soviet behavior in southern Africa demonstrates what the Kremlin can do far from its periphery, in a region where Moscow has important, if not vital, interests. What is remarkable is the extent to which the USSR has been willing to facilitate violence there, despite considerable rhetoric to the contrary.

Moscow's policy in southern Africa is global in that over time the Kremlin has employed its worldwide assets to support its initiatives in this region and to enhance its relative influence around the globe.[28] A few examples suffice. The Portuguese Communists helped the Kremlin penetrate the MPLA; Cubans helped train Mozambique's army. The portrayal of the United States as a bulwark of apartheid, however unwarranted, garners support in many corners of the world and stimulates divisions in U.S. society, as the 1988 presidential election indicated. African minerals relieve pressure on the USSR to subsidize its Eastern European empire. The North Vietnamese advise the Angolan army on resisting siege tactics and in 1988 and 1989 began replacing the 13,000 Cuban technical advisers. These are but a few examples of this global policy, which mirrors the interdependence of Moscow's global empire.

Moscow's policy is also global in that regional conflicts have become bargaining chips in the relations between superpowers. For example, at the June 1988 summit meeting in the United States, the chief new agreement between Moscow and Washington was that efforts to arrive at an accommodation in Angola should be pursued. Put another way, Soviet involvement in southern Africa provided the USSR with leverage to barter for U.S. concessions in other arenas.

The Kremlin's policy is global in a third sense. The magnitude of Soviet involvement—like that of the Russian Empire before it—is conditioned by other priorities, like the arms race and economic reform. However, the constraining influence of the financial costs of Soviet involvement in southern Africa should not be overestimated. The cost of aiding the ANC is minimal. Much of the cost of the Angolan intervention was underwritten by payment in hard currency for weapons, currency that the USSR finds difficult to earn in other ways, a dramatic difference from the Afghanistan or Ethiopian interventions.

Analysts disagree on how much Angola owes the USSR and how much it has actually paid. NATO estimates that Moscow received approximately $8.1 billion from Angola from 1978 to 1988.[29] Christopher Coker puts this figure at $15.5 billion between 1978 and 1983, but suggests that the Kremlin may not have been paid for all of this.³⁰ He points out that Angola managed to pay half its foreign debt to the USSR in the summer of 1987 before the fall of oil prices. The Soviets also exploited the fishing resources of the region and rigged the terms of trade in unfavorable ways to mitigate the costs of involvement.

Nevertheless, cost is a factor. Until the late 1980s Angola paid for much of its aid in scarce hard currency, and the proportion of the Soviet defense budget allocated to that country was small. The USSR did reschedule payments for military assistance, but, after all, these were credits, not gifts. Although Angola's economy is in ruins, its mineral resources are substantial, which suggests that Moscow ultimately will be repaid. The devastation in the Afro-Marxist states and the exorbitant cost of increasingly high-tech weapons may serve to restrain Soviet initiatives somewhat in the short run. After oil prices rose, Moscow was forced to roll over much of Angola's debt, two-thirds of which is owed to the USSR.³¹ But in the long run, given the record of Soviet resourcefulness and the global political benefits accruing from past involvement, such constraint is far from certain.

What is certain is that Moscow's influence in southern Africa rests on a dramatically higher plane than it did at the Sixth Comintern Conference in 1928, when an American Communist delegate asked why the Communist-led revolutionary forces in Mozambique had attempted without success to establish contact with the Comintern. The delegate went on to question why more had not been done by the "Propaganda Commission" to promote revolution in Africa.³²

Much has changed. After almost two decades of massive involvement in southern Africa, Soviet behavior indicates that the USSR is unlikely to abandon Lenin's caveat: "It is evident that in the decisive battles of the world revolution the movements of the colonial peoples will play a greater revolutionary role then we dare hope." ³³ Both the Soviets and the ANC often refer to the South African political system as colonialism of a special kind.³⁴

Soviet involvement in southern Africa has been part of a larger strategy to engage the United States in marginal areas where the risks of significant confrontation were perceived to be relatively minimal, thereby distracting its superpower adversary, in a cost-effective way, from devoting full attention to areas of vital interest. If renewal at home and an improvement in Soviet-U.S. relations are serious objectives of Gorbachev, then some amelioration of this strategy is imperative. But his regime is constrained by a political culture conditioned to pursuing a policy of probing for influence in the Third World; thus the prospects for a dramatic change in strategy are dim, though not completely negligible.³⁵ Although the peripheral nature of southern Africa to vital superpower interests suggests that it might be an auspicious locus for Soviet-U.S. cooperation, it is equally probable that precisely because of its marginality old patterns will persist, with perhaps a more vigorous political component, especially given the perceived public diplomacy opportunities.[36] However, it is certainly not inconceivable in the climate of *perestroika* and with the release of Nelson Mandela that continued persistent and patient diplomacy and mediation could yield more cooperative Soviet-American initiatives, facilitating the attenuation of the conflicts in the region.

NOTES

Chapter 1

1. *Pravda,* May 18, 1984, p. 1.
2. The chief proponent and architect of Gorbachev's public diplomacy is Alexander N. Yakovlev, a CPSU secretary and new head of the CPSU Foreign Affairs Commission. He is known to be fiercely anti-American. His seminal article is "Sources of the Threat and Public Opinion," *Mirovaya Ekonomika i Mezhdunarodyye Otnosheniya* (hereinafter cited as *MEMO*), March 1985. It describes what has emerged as the Gorbachev public diplomacy strategy. The standard Soviet line is spelled out in Andrei I. Urnov (then head of the southern Africa section of the International Department of the Soviet Communist Party), "Al' ians Vashington-Pretoria i Afrika," *MEMO,* March 1983. On the institutionalized orchestration of Soviet public diplomacy, see Richard F. Staar, ed., *Public Diplomacy: USA Versus USSR* (Stanford: Hoover Institution Press, 1986); and Richard Shultz and Roy Godson, *Dezinformatsia: Active Measures in Soviet Strategy* (Washington: Pergamon Brassey's, 1984).
3. At the time, Kirilenko was regarded as Brezhnev's most likely successor. He headed the powerful national security committee of the ruling Politburo.
4. V. G. Solodovnikov, *The Years of the Africa Institute: Scientific Achievements and Tasks of Soviet African Studies,* Studies on Developing Countries, no. 55 (Budapest: Hungarian Academy of Sciences, Center for Afro-Asian Research, 1971).
5. Potekhin's diary for this visit is *Gana Segodnia* (Moscow: Progress Publishers, 1958).
6. Boris A. Asoyan, "A Soviet Diplomat's View of South Africa," *South Africa Foundation Review* (June 1988): 7, gives an abbreviated version of one of these lectures.
7. Reflecting Y. A. Primakov's competitive geopolitical mind-set, in which he seems eager to engage the United States if it will not cooperate, are his following works: "Osvobodivshiesia strany v mezhdunarodnykh otnosheniiakh," *MEMO* (May 1980): 22; "Zakon neravnomernosti razvitiia i istoricheskie syd'by osvobodivshikhsia stran," *MEMO* (December 1980): 38; and "Strany sotsialisti-

cheskoi orientatsii: trudnyi, no real'nyi perekhod k sotisalizmu," *MEMO* (July 1981): 11.

8. Vernon Aspaturian, "The Soviet Foreign Policy Apparatus" (*Meeting Report*, Kennan Institute for Advanced Russian Studies, The Wilson Center, November 16, 1987), p. 1.

9. Information on the Soviet personnel involved in the southern African decision-making process is drawn from Diplomaticheskii Slovar, *USSR Ministry of Foreign Affairs: A Reference Aid* (Washington: CIA, September 1987); *Foreign Broadcast Information Service* (hereinafter cited as *FBIS*); and *Soviet Revue*, among others.

10. See Urnov, "Al'ians Vashington-Pretoria i Afrika," for his exposition of the Soviet public diplomacy position.

11. Slovar, *USSR Ministry*, pp. 22–23; and Claire Rosenson, "Personnel Changes in the Ministry of Foreign Affairs," *Sovset*, July 9, 1986, pp. 13–14.

12. As Richard F. Staar demonstrated, Dybenko was one of only 22 CPSU Central Committee members in 1986 who held ambassadorial appointments (*USSR Foreign Policies After Detente*, rev. ed. [Stanford: Hoover Institution Press: 1987], p. 51).

13. William Pascoe, "Moscow's Strategy in Southern Africa," *The Backgrounder*, July 21, 1986.

14. *Africa Insider,* July 15–31, 1987, p. 6.

15. *Soviet Revue*, July–August 1987, pp. 12–13.

16. *Economist,* May 28, 1988, p. 39.

17. Ibid.

18. *New York Times,* September 26, 1987, p. 8, reports Nel's visit. See Steven Friedman and Monty Narsoo, *A New Mood in Moscow: Soviet Attitudes to South Africa* (Johannesburg: South African Institute of Race Relations, 1989), p. 8. On previous Soviet ambivalence, see Peter Vanneman and W. Martin James III, "The Role of Opinion Groups in the Soviet African Policy Process," *Journal of Contemporary African Studies* 2, no. 2 (1983): 211.

19. Christopher Coker, "Soviet Bloc Economic Interests in Southern Africa," *Soviet Revue*, March–April 1988, p. 10.

20. For the South African account of KGB activities, see Henry R. Pike, *A History of Communism in South Africa* (Germiston: Christian Mission International of South Africa, 1985). For summary of Western sources, see Kurt Campbell, *Soviet Policy Towards South Africa* (New York: St. Martin's Press, 1986), pp. 127–40.

21. Richard F. Staar, "Checklist of Communist Parties and Fronts, 1981," *Problems of Communism,* January–February 1982, p. 71, lists the political parties and movements that Moscow views as critical elements in the National Liberation Movement.

22. *Washington Post,* December 3, 1983, p. 1.

23. On Soviet disinformation with respect to alleged U.S.–South African collusion

over UNITA, see Moscow Radio (in English) *FBIS-Sov,* August 2, 1984, p. u/1 (translated from Zulu); and Moscow Radio (in English) *FBIS-Sov,* June 3, 1985, p. u/1.
24. *Economist,* May 28, 1988, p. 39.
25. Yakovlev, "Sources of the Threat," pp. 10–13.
26. Thomas Henriksen, ed., *Communist Powers and Sub-Saharan Africa* (Stanford: Hoover Institution Press, 1981), p. 124.
27. Karen Brutents, "Osvobadivshiesya strany v nachale 80-kh godov," *Kommunist,* no. 3 (February 1984): 109.
28. Peter Sullivan, "The Soviet Union: A Personal View," *South Africa Foundation Review* (November 1988): 7.
29. As Yuri Yukalov, head of the Africa Department of the Soviet Foreign Ministry, put it, "It is still untimely to announce the establishment of diplomatic relations. . . . Such relations will become possible only if South Africa . . . implements . . . radical changes." *Soviet Revue,* March–April 1989, p. 26. See also Professor Apollon Davidson, Institute of World History, USSR Academy of Sciences, African Department, "The USSR and the Angola/Namibia Accords" (Address to Fourth International Conference Institute for Soviet and East European Studies, University of Miami, December 20, 1988).
30. *New York Times,* December 14, 1988, p. 6. The invitation is in Article 3 of the Annex to the Agreement.
31. Interview with Yuri Yukalov, *Soviet Revue,* March–April, p. 26.

Chapter 2

1. *Congress Voice,* February 1961, p. 13; Edward Feit, *Urban Revolt in South Africa* (Evanston, Ill.: Northwestern University Press, 1971), p. 119; Tom Lodge, *Black Politics in South Africa Since 1945* (Johannesburg: Ravan Press, 1985), pp. 233–35. See also L. H. Gann and Peter Duignan, *Why South Africa Will Survive: A Historical Analysis* (New York: St. Martin's Press, 1981),pp. 236–53.
2. Peter Duignan, "Africa from a Globalist Perspective," in Gerald Bender, ed., *African Crisis Areas and U.S. Foreign Policy* (Los Angeles: African Studies Center, UCLA, 1985), p. 294.
3. *Pravda,* July 16, 1987, p. 4. This article discusses a meeting between Afrikaner intellectuals and liberals, and the ANC in Dakar.
4. Radio Moscow, August 30, 1987, *FBIS-Sov* (in Russian), September 7, 1987, p. cc12.
5. Gleb Starushenko, "For Peace, Cooperation and Social Progress" (Paper to Second Soviet-African Scientific Political Conference, Moscow, June 1986).
6. The new alliance, "popular front," strategy is outlined in detail by the director of the Africa Institute in Anatoly Gromyko, "Pokonchit's Rasistmom i Kolinializmom," *Azia i Afrika Segodnia* (March 1986): 7–9.

7. *Soviet Revue,* November–December 1988, p. 27. The role of white liberals in the revolutionary process is also analyzed in detail in B. Bogdanov, "Treschiny v monolite ili vzorvannyi mif," *Azia i Afrika Segodnia* (April 1986): 24–28.
8. Michael Radu, "African National Congress: Cadres and Credo," *Problems of Communism,* July–August 1987, p. 58. According to Stephen Davis, the ANC leadership makes decisions by majority vote requiring a quorum (*Apartheid's Rebels: Inside South Africa's Hidden War* [New Haven: Yale University Press, 1987], p. 50.
9. Davis, *Apartheid's Rebels,* pp. 9, 10.
10. *Africa Confidential,* May 27, 1988, pp. 3, 4 describes the contest within the unions in some detail.
11. *Africa Confidential,* August 12, 1988, pp. 1, 3.
12. *Washington Post,* in *AFP Press Clips,* July 15, 1988, p. 7.
13. Interview with Steve Tswete, *Baltimore Sun,* November 24, 1987, in *AFP Press Clips,* November 24, 1987, p. 3; interview with Chris Hani, *New York Times* (international edition), June 12, 1988, p. 4; *Foreign Report,* March 17, 1988, p. 5.
14. *Foreign Report,* June 2, 1988, p. 3, describes the secret meeting, details of which were leaked to the press.
15. *Foreign Report,* June 30, 1988, p. 5.
16. *New York Times,* July 7, 1988, p. 4.
17. *New York Times,* October 25, 1988, p. 4.
18. *Washington Post,* February 26, 1988, in *AFP Press Clips,* February 26, 1988, p. 5.
19. Boris Asoyan, "A Soviet Diplomat's View of South Africa," *South Africa Foundation Review* (June 1988): 7.
20. BBC "Review of World Events," SU8265/A5/1, May 22, 1986.
21. *Washington Times,* November 7, 1986, in *AFP Press Clips,* November 7, 1986, p. 5.
22. Ibid.
23. *Soviet Revue* (November–December 1988) and Davis, *Apartheid's Rebels,* 16.
24. Chester Crocker, assistant secretary of state for African affairs, *The Role of the Soviet Union, Cuba, and East Germany in Fomenting Terrorism in Southern Africa,* hearings before the Subcommittee on Security and Terrorism of the Committee on the Judiciary, U.S. Senate, 97th Congress, March 22, 1981, vol. 1, Serial no. J-97–101, p. 7; *South Africa Time Running Out,* report of the Study Commission on U.S. Policy Toward Southern Africa (Berkeley: University of California Press, 1981), p. 204.
25. *Pravda,* January 8, 1987; and *Pravda,* January 4, 1987. On rumored Nigerian aid, see *Africa Confidential,* July 16, 1986, p. 7.
26. Mark A. Uhlig, "Inside the African National Congress," *New York Times Magazine,* October 12, 1986, in *AFP Press Clips,* October 16, 1986, p. 5.

27. *The Star* (Johannesburg), October 14, 1979, cited by Tom Lodge, "The African National Congress in South Africa, 1976–1983: Guerrilla War and Armed Propaganda," *Journal of Contemporary African Studies* 3, no. 1–2 (October 1983–April 1984): 166.
28. Davis, *Apartheid's Rebels*, pp. 70–71, called the Soviet-made arsenal obsolete, but *Africa Confidential*, July 15, 1988, p. 5, reported the discovery of an ANC cell with plans to use the SAM-7 against military and police aircraft inside South Africa.
29. *Africa Confidential*, December 10, 1986, p. 1.
30. "Communist Weapons for African Rebels," *Christian Science Monitor*, March 11, 1987, in *AFP Press Clips*, March 13, 1987, p. 3.
31. Ibid.
32. *Financial Mail* (South Africa), March 19, 1983, pp. 17, 18.
33. *Le Figaro*, September 5, 1981, p. 5; *Jane's Defense Weekly*, March 23, 1985, p. 490.
34. Carole A. Douglis and Stephen M. Davis, "Revolt on the Veldt," *Harper's*, December 1983, p. 37, based on interviews at ANC camp at Mazimbu, Tanzania.
35. "Communist Weapons for African Rebels," *Christian Science Monitor*, March 11, 1987, in *AFP Press Clips*, March 13, 1987, p. 3.
36. *Financial Mail* (South Africa), June 10, 1983, pp. 3–4.
37. *New York Times*, June 24, 1986, p. 1.
38. In 1989 South African security estimated 6,000 (*Africa Confidential*, January 20, 1989, p. 6). The ANC figure comes from James North, whose pen name is Daniel Swanson. He lived in South Africa for four years, at times working underground with the ANC. See *Washington Post*, March 9, 1986, in *AFP Press Clips*, March 14, 1986, p. 5. See also "Inside the ANC," *Foreign Report*, February 13, 1986, p. 1. The South African security apparatus gave the 4,000 figure in *Rand Daily Mail* (Johannesburg), June 2, 1978, p. 3.
39. See J. Barrat, *The Soviet Union and South Africa*, (occasional paper, Johannesburg: South African Institute of International Affairs), p. 17, which cites a captured KGB agent, Major Kozlov; and I. A. Ulanovskaia, *South Africa: Racism Doomed* (Moscow: Znanie, 1978), p. 41, which refers disdainfully to "the lack of experiences by the patriots in revolutionary actions."
40. *Economist*, July 26, 1985, p. 35; Thomas Lodge, "The Second Consultative Conference of the African National Congress," *South Africa International* 16, no. 2 (October 1985): 93. However, the South African government identified Modise as a Communist in *Talking with the ANC* (Pretoria: Bureau of Information, 1986), p. 14.
41. *Talking with the ANC*, p. 14, identifies Slovo as a KGB colonel. The author has not seen any evidence of this formal link; however, Slovo has been a Communist since 1940. See his biography in Shelagh Gastrow, *Who Is Who in South African Politics* (Johannesburg: Ravan Press, 1985), p. 291. He helped found the *Umkhonto* and has served on its military planning committees since 1969. He is the

ANC's foremost revolutionary theorist and military thinker, according to Lodge, "Second Consultative Conference," p. 94. According to Jorge da Costa, the former chief of Mozambique's national security apparatus who defected to South Africa, "There is no doubt in my mind that Slovo is behind every operation launched by the ANC against South Africa. He has a brilliant mind and is one of the best-informed people about this country." Craig Williamson, a South African security agent who infiltrated the ANC from 1971–1980, characterizes Slovo as "the classic South African communist that the Soviets like—tough down the line, disciplined and utterly dedicated." (*Scope Magazine* [South Africa], February 25, 1985, p. 18. Slovo considers any suggestion that he is a Soviet puppet as a "slanderous insult." (*Time,* March 2, 1987, p. 36).
Moscow Radio (in English), *FBIS-Sov,* May 30, 1984, p. CC 12.

42. *Washington Times,* April 22, 1987, in *AFP Press Clips,* April 24, 1986, p. 10; and *Foreign Report,* February 5, 1987, p. 4.
43. *Africa Confidential,* August 12, 1988, p. 3.
44. *Washington Post,* December 7, 1987, in *AFP Press Clips,* December 11, 1987, p. 1.
45. *Weekly Mail* (South Africa), June 12, 1987, pp. 3–4.
46. *Washington Post,* March 15, 1988, pp. 2–3. According to the South African government, senior Soviet officials approached lower level South African officials.
47. Allister Sparks, "Moscow's New Game in Africa," *New York Times,* October 3, 1988, in *AFP Press Clips,* October 14, 1988, p. 4.
48. *Africa Confidential,* August 26, 1988, pp. 1–3.
49. *New York Times,* March 16, 1989, p. 1.
50. Richard Staar, *USSR Foreign Policies After Détente,* rev. ed. (Stanford: Hoover Institution Press, 1987), p. 13.

Chapter 3

1. The U.S. State Department's confidential report to Congress apparently provides a balanced and solid analysis that does not rely merely on counting Communists on the 30-member ruling National Executive Council (NEC) of the ANC: "Roughly half the 30 members are known or *suspected* SACP (South African Communist Party) members ... but evidence of SACP membership is not conclusive in several cases" [emphasis added] (*New York Times,* January 9, 1987, p. 2). The *Economist,* July 26, 1986, p. 35, reported that at least ten were SACP "and perhaps as many as 14 or 15." The *Economist,* January 31, 1987, p. 15, estimated "up to half" were SACP.

   Foreign diplomats in South Africa estimate that one-third are Communists, but South African President P. W. Botha says 63 percent (Patti Waldmeir, "The

African National Congress," *Financial Times* [South Africa], May 21, 1986, pp. 4–5).

A white South African academic specialist sympathetic to the ANC argues that "about half the executive are members of the SACP," and this has been the case for some time (Thomas Lodge, "The Second Consultative Conference of the African National Congress," *South Africa International* 16, no. 2 [October 1985]: 95). Congressman Dan Burton, a Republican from Indiana, inserted into the *Congressional Record* a list allegedly compiled by the staff of Senator Jeremiah Denton, Republican from Alabama, from South African intelligence sources, among others. Burton's list concluded that "at least 19 and possibly 25 are known communists, although it is not in all cases possible to give documentary proof of SACP membership" (*Congressional Record*, H3901, June 19, 1986). In June 1986 the Bureau for Information of the South African government published a pamphlet, *Talking with the ANC*, using the broad definition of communism in that nation's Terrorism Act, alleging on page 14 that 23 were Communists. A declassified CIA report estimates that 18 are Communists (*Congressional Record*, August 14, 1986, pp. S11655–656, S11660–661). But an American academic specialist on the ANC argues that only three of them are actually Communists (Thomas G. Karis, "South African Liberation: The Communist Factor," *Foreign Affairs* [winter 1986/1987]: 281). *Africa Confidential*, August 26, 1988, p. 3, estimates 22 of 28, before the July 1988 reshuffle, and 25 of 35 after it.

2. The Comprehensive Anti-Apartheid Act of 1986. Public Law 99–440, October 2, 1986, sec. 509a, 100 Stat. 1111.

3. Andrei I. Urnov, "The South African Knot," *Mirovaya Ekonomika i Mezhdunarodnyye Otnosheniya* (hereinafter cited as *MEMO*), no. 5 (May 1984): 118–21. As head of the Southern Africa Division of the International Department of the Soviet Communist Party, Urnov is a key policy adviser. See also Ivan A. Ulanovakaia, "The Labor Movement in the R.S.A.," *Narodny Azii i Afriki*, no. 2 (March–April 1978): 27, expressing the innate fear that labor reform could siphon off revolutionary fervor among workers; and S. Burlitsky, "R.S.A.: Crisis of Racist Regime," *Aziia i Afrika segodnia* (September 1977): 20. Private conversations with Soviet Africanists confirm the uneasiness; see Robert Legvold, "The Soviet Threat to Southern Africa," in Robert I. Rotberg, ed., *South Africa and Its Neighbors: Regional Security and Self-Interest* (Lexington, Mass.: Greenwood Press, 1985), pp. 41, 42.

4. BBC "Review of World Events," SU8265/A5/1, May 22, 1986.

5. Tom Karis, "Revolution in the Making: Black Politics in South Africa," *Foreign Affairs* 62, no. 2 (winter 1983/1984): 281–93.

6. *Washington Post*, March 9, 1986, in *AFP Press Clips*, March 14, 1986, p. 5.

7. *Foreign Report*, June 30, 1988, p. 5.

8. *The Star* (Johannesburg), January 7, 1982; *New York Times*, June 24, 1986, p. 1.

9. *Foreign Report,* February 13, 1986, p. 2.
10. *New York Times,* June 24, 1986, p. 1. The *Sunday Observer,* May 24, 1987, p. 15, reports that "the Russian AK-47 rifle has become talismanic," somewhat like the Red flag unfurled at rallies.
11. *South Africa Digest,* March 14, 1986, p. 210.
12. *International Herald Tribune,* November 5, 1982, p. 75, cites a CIA report to this effect; see also *Race Relations Survey, 1984,* p. 27 (Johannesburg: South African Institute of Race Relations [a private liberal think tank]); and *Newsweek,* September 6, 1985, p. 13.
13. Richard Gibson, *African Liberation Movements: Contemporary Struggle Against White Minority Rule* (Oxford: Oxford University Press, 1971), p. 64.
14. This is persuasively argued in J. H. Billington, *Fire in the Minds of Men* (New York: Harper and Row, 1980), p. 462, citing V. I. Lenin, *What Is to Be Done?* (Moscow: Novosti, n.d.), pp. 40–44 and 58–60.
15. *Guardian,* July 22, 1985, p. 17.
16. V. I. Lenin, *Gosudartsvo i revoliutsiia, Polnoe Sobranie,* Vol. no. 33 of the *Collected Works* (Moscow: Progress Publishers, 1974). pp. 48, 91.
17. *Africa Confidential,* July 3, 1985, p. 73.
18. Ibid., p. 1. This is the implication of the word *leadership* in the last paragraph.
19. *Guardian,* July 22, 1985, pp. 1–6. Reiterated in summer 1986, see *Africa Confidential,* August 20, 1986, p. 8. For a description of the communication system, see "Marnet on the Alert," *South Africa Digest,* July 4, 1986, p. 616.
20. See "The ANC's Secret Decisions," *Foreign Report,* July 4, 1985, p. 5.
21. Ibid.; see also Thomas Lodge, The Second Consultative Conference of the African National Congress, *South Africa International* 16, no. 2 (October 1985): especially pp. 86, 87.
22. *Sunday Times* (London), September 8, 1985, p. 14.
23. *Race Relations Survey,* p. 95 (see n. 12).
24. See the prominent American Africanist, William R. Cotter, "It's the Leading Black Political Group," *Washington Post,* July 20, 1986, in *AFP Press Clips,* July 25, 1986, pp. 9, 14. For example, see Conor Cruise O'Brien, "What Can Become of South Africa," *Atlantic Monthly,* March 1986, p. 43: "The guillotine was merciful compared with the children's chosen method of execution: burning alive, with a gasoline-filled tire, 'the necklace,' around one's neck."
25. Cotter, "Leading Black Political Group," p. 9, states that "some of its [the ANC's] people practice necklacing—the terrible killings of other blacks."
26. *New York Times,* May 14, 1987, in *AFP Press Clips,* May 15, 1987, p. 1; he is quoted in *Foreign Report,* October 2, 1986, p. 6.
27. *Economist,* July 1, 1988, p. 47.
28. *Africa Confidential,* July 15, 1988, p. 4.
29. For one SACP version of its relationship with the ANC, see the article in the Soviet Communist Party's theoretical journal by the late SACP secretary general,

Moses Mabhida, "In the Struggle for National and Social Liberation of the People," *Kommunist*, no. 11 (June 1981): 23, which claims that ANC and SACP decisions are made "jointly." The ANC denies that the SACP exercises such a leading role. As ANC President Oliver Tambo put it, "They [the SACP] all owe their primary allegiance to the ANC" (*Washington Post*, March 7, 1986, in *AFP Press Clips*, March 7, 1986, p. 16).

At a 1986 SACP rally, ANC Secretary-General Alfred Nzo and then SACP Chairman Joe Slovo reportedly referred to the ANC as "the 'propellant' in an array of organizations dedicated to bringing down the government" (*New York Times*, August 1, 1986, p. 14).

Previously Joe Slovo stated, "The SACP is part of the broad liberation front headed by the ANC." He went on to talk about "the SACP's *independent* role as well as its role within the Alliance" [emphasis added]. A major facet of this independent role is "the lifegiving relationship between our movement as a whole and the progressive forces throughout the world, and *particularly in the socialist countries.* This is something we have always cherished and will safeguard in the future" [emphasis added] (*World Marxist Review* [October 1985]: 57).

30. Robert Monroe, "Trade Union Organization in the South African Revolution," *Marxist Workers Tendency* (London), no. 1 (January 1981), cited in Andrew Prior, "South African Exile Politics: The ANC and SACP," *Journal of Contemporary African Studies* 3, no. 1–2 (1983–1984): 192.

31. For a detailed example of this line, see Andrei I. Urnov (head of the Southern Africa Division of the International Department of the Soviet Communist Party), "Al'ians Vashington-Pretoria i Afrika," *MEMO* (March 1983).

As the late Soviet leader Chernenko put it: "A complex situation is now developing in southern Africa, where the South African racist regime with the connivance of the United States believes itself entitled to ignore the resolutions of the U.N. Security Council on independence for Namibia . . . [T]he United States and some of its allies are striving to impose their wishes on the people of southern Africa" (*Krasnaya Zvezda* [Moscow: Red Star], May 30, 1984, p. 11). Fidel Castro in a long front-page editorial in *Granma,* his party newspaper, called the "U.S.-South African axis" a pair of "freebooters" (*Washington Post,* May 30, 1985, p. A23).

This theme is central to articles by the two recent chairmen of the SACP, see Dan Tloome, "Foul Play by the Pretoria Regime," *World Marxist Review* (July 1986): especially pp. 31, 32; and *Guardian,* July 16, 1985, p. 58.

On the elaborate institutionalized orchestration of Soviet propaganda, see Richard Shultz and Roy Godsen, *Dezinformatsia: Active Measures in Soviet Strategy* (Washington: Pergamon-Brassey's, 1984), pp. 1–197.

32. Prior, "Exile Politics," p. 192.
33. Ibid.
34. Ibid.
35. Ibid.

36. Kurt Campbell, "The Soviet-South African Connection," *Africa Report* (March–April 1986): 72–75; and Campbell, *Soviet Policy Towards South Africa* (New York: St. Martin's Press, 1986) chap. 5.
37. *Reuters,* July 16, 1984, p. 7, interview quoting American Africanist Helen Kitchen on conversations with Soviet academics.
38. David Albright, "New Trends in Soviet Policy Toward Africa," *CSIS Africa Notes,* no. 27, April 29, 1984, pp. 7, 8.
39. Colin Legum, "International Rivalries in the Southern African Conflict," in Gwendolyn Carter and Patrick O'Meary, eds., *Southern Africa: The Continuing Crisis* (London: Macmillan, 1979), p. 17.
40. Gibson, *African Liberation Movements,* pp. 65–105. Professor Vanneman observed the early phases of this struggle firsthand in Tanzania in 1966–1967 while serving on the staff of President Julius Nyerere.
41. Thomas Lodge, "The African National Congress in South Africa, 1976–1983, Guerrilla War and Armed Propaganda," *Journal of Contemporary African Studies* 3, no. 1–2 (October 1983–April 1984): 166.
42. The following biographical data are based on confidential interviews and *Africa Confidential,* December 11, 1985, pp. 1–5, and *Africa Confidential,* July 3, 1985, pp. 1 and 2.
43. Karis, "Revolution in the Making," p. 283.
44. See *Africa Insider,* June 15, 1986, p. 2; and Frances Meli, "On the Spectrum of the ANC's Struggle in Southern Africa," *UCLA African Studies Newsletter* (spring 1986): 26–32.
45. *Foreign Report,* February 13, 1986, p. 2; and *Christian Science Monitor,* April 16, 1986, pp. 26–32.
46. *Christian Science Monitor,* April 16, 1988, pp. 26–32.
47. Mark A. Uhlig, "Inside the African National Congress," *New York Times Magazine,* October 12, 1986, p. 4; and Carole A. Douglis and Stephen M. Davis, "Revolt on the Veldt," *Harper's,* December 1983, p. 35.
48. *Argus* (Capetown, South Africa), August 11, 1989, p. 14. The quote is from a review of Boris Asoyan, *South Africa: What Lies Ahead* (Moscow: Novosti Press, 1989).
49. *Soviet Revue,* May–June 1989, p. 35–36.

Chapter 4

1. *Pravda,* May 18, 1984, p. 1.
2. See V. Iu. Vasil'kov, "Problema Namibii i positsiia SShA," *SShA: politika, ekonomika, ideologiia,* no. 4 (1983): 49–52.
3. Moscow Radio (in English), *FBIS-Sov,* May 30, 1984, p. CC 12.
4. *Pravda,* October 10, 1984, p. 2.

5. *New York Times,* July 28, 1988, p. 5, estimates between 10,000 and 15,000; *Jane's Defense Weekly,* June 11, 1988, p. 1132, gives the 10,000 figure; UNITA reported 9,000 (*Free Angola Information Service,* June 13, 1988, p. 1); *Foreign Report,* June 9, 1988, p. 3, estimates between 5,000 and 8,000; *Africa Confidential,* May 27, 1988, p. 1, talks of "thousands of Cuban reinforcements, who have arrived by sea"; Angola confirmed the reinforcements but gave no figures (*Jane's Defense Weekly,* June 4, 1988, p. 1100).
6. *New York Times,* July 28, 1988, p. 5, gives the 50,000 figure; *Foreign Report,* June 9, 1988, p. 3, reports new troops joining the "45,000 or so Cubans already there."
7. *New York Times,* May 31, 1988, in *AFP Press Clips,* June 3, 1988, p. 5.
8. *Washington Times,* June 6, 1988, p. A10.
9. *New York Times,* May 17, 1988, in *AFP Press Clips,* May 20, 1988, p. 5.
10. See Gillian Gunn, "Cuba and Angola," *CSIS Africa Notes,* no. 20, March 31, 1987, p. 2. Apparently, the Angolans were not happy about Castro wanting to stay so long.
11. *New York Times,* May 17, 1988, in *AFP Press Clips,* May 20, 1988, p. 5.
12. *Jane's Defense Weekly,* July 9, 1988, p. 24.
13. *New York Times,* July 28, 1988, p. 5; and *Jane's Defense Weekly,* June 4, 1988, p. 1100.
14. *Jane's Defense Weekly,* June 4, 1988, p. 1100.
15. Ibid.
16. *Jane's Defense Weekly,* July 9, 1988, p. 24, and the *Economist,* July 2, 1988, p. 37, describe the battle at the dam.
17. *Sunday Times* (London), June 19, 1988, p. 10.
18. *Africa Confidential,* May 27, 1988, p. 1.
19. Richard Gibson, *African Liberation Movements: Contemporary Struggle Against White Minority Rule* (Oxford: Oxford University Press, 1971), p. 135, and the chapter on southwest Africa (pp. 195–221); and Keith Somerville, "The Soviet Union and Zimbabwe: The Liberation Struggle and After," in R. C. Nation and M. V. Kauppi, eds., *The Soviet Impact on Africa* (Lexington, Mass.: Lexington Books, 1984), p. 199.
20. Somerville, "Soviet Union and Zimbabwe," p. 199.
21. *Le Figaro,* September 5, 1981, p. 4, reports 100 SWAPO trainees returning to Angola from East Germany and 90 arriving in Berlin; *Jane's Defense Weekly,* March 23, 1985, p. 490, reports 120 SWAPO returning from Berlin after a three-year program.
22. *Africa Confidential,* May 27, 1987, p. 4.
23. First estimate: Peter Vanneman and Martin James III, *Soviet Foreign Policy in Southern Africa: Problems and Prospects* (Pretoria, Africa Institute of South Africa, 1982), p. 47; second estimate: L. H. Gann, "The U.S.S.R., the West and South Africa," *Strategic Review* (September 1984): 24 (Gann gives the 8,000

figure); third estimate: *Economist,* March 30, 1985, p. 22, puts SWAPO at 8,500 with 80 percent in southern Angola.

24. Andre du Pisani provides an excellent summary of the bush war and the negotiations surrounding it in "SWA/Namibia Update: 1981 to April 1984," *Africa Insight* 14, no. 3 (1984): 176; see especially p. 187. *Jane's Defense Weekly,* June 8, 1985, p. 1053, reports 302 SWAPO fatalities from January until May 1985.
25. du Pisani, "SWA/Namibia Update," p. 179.
26. Ibid., p. 184.
27. *U.N. Chronicle* 20 no. 3 (March 1983): 28.
28. du Pisani, "SWA/Namibia Update," pp. 184–85.
29. Ibid.
30. *Jane's Defense Weekly,* March 23, 1985, p. 490.
31. du Pisani, "SWA/Namibia Update," p. 189.
32. *Economist,* March 30, 1985, p. 21; du Pisani, "SWA/Namibia Update," p. 189.
33. Ian Smiley, "Inside Angola," *New York Review of Books,* February 17, 1983, pp. 13–14.
34. The *Guardian,* October 29, 1983, cited in Christopher Coker, *NATO, the Warsaw Pact and Africa* (London: Macmillan, 1984), p. 246.
35. *Jane's Defense Weekly,* April 2, 1988, p. 615.
36. On factionalism in SWAPO, see V. Shubin, "Maneuvers of the Racists Doomed to Failure," *Aziia i Afrika Segodnia,* no. 6 (June 1977): 17. The author identifies five factions in SWAPO: those in Zambia, in Angola, in Namibia (operating legally), guerrillas in Namibia, and émigrés elsewhere. On arms see Chester Crocker, U.S. assistant secretary of state for Africa, *The Role of the Soviet Union, Cuba, and East Germany in Fomenting Terrorism,* hearings before the Subcommittee on Security and Terrorism, of the Committee on the Judiciary, 97th Congress, March 21, 1982, p. 7.
37. Gibson, *African Liberation Movements,* p. 134.
38. Sam Nujoma, "My uvereny v svoiei pobede" [We believe in our victory], *Kommunist* (November 1980): 105–6.
39. du Pisani, "SWA/Namibia Update," p. 190.
40. Vittorfranco S. Pisano, "Conflict in the Southern African Region," *Clandestine Tactics and Technology* 10, no. 7 (April 1983): 4.
41. This is according to a captured Soviet spy, Major Kozlov, in John Barrat, *The Soviet Union and Southern Africa* (Occasional Paper, The South African Institute of International Affairs), p. 17.
42. Colin Legum, "The Southern African Crisis," in Colin Legum, ed., *Africa Contemporary Record,* 1981–82 (New York: Africana Publishers, 1982), p. 43.
43. *New York Times,* July 6, 1988, in *AFP Press Clips,* July 17, 1988, p. 5.
44. *Africa Confidential,* March 17, 1989, p. 3; and *New York Times,* April 27, 1989, in *AFP Press Clips,* April 28, 1989, p. 2.
45. *Washington Times,* May 1, 1989, in *AFP Press Clips,* May 5, 1989, p. 14.

Chapter 5

1. *New York Times*, September 27, 1987, p. 8; and TASS (Moscow), March 31, 1986. Gorbachev's speech at a dinner for Mozambique's late president Samora Machel conveys the same message.
2. Mikhail S. Gorbachev, *Political Report of the CPSU Central Committee to the 27th Party Congress* (Moscow, 1986), p. 87.
3. Alexander N. Yakovlev, "Sources of the Threat and Public Opinion," *MEMO* (March 1985).
4. All sources agree that a large contingent of fresh Cuban combat troops arrived by sea at the port of Namibe in southern Angola between May and June 1988 and were deployed near the Namibian border. *Foreign Report*, June 9, 1988, p. 3, puts the total figure at 45,000 "or so"; The *New York Times*, June 6, 1988, p. 4, reported 40,000; UNITA reported 50,000 in *Free Angola Information Service*, June 13, 1988, p. 1; *Africa Confidential*, May 27, 1988, p. 1, reported "thousands of Cuban reinforcements . . . have arrived." *Jane's Defense Weekly*, June 11, 1988, p. 1132, reported 10,000 Cubans deployed on the Namibian border.
5. On the broader political aspects of the Angolan intervention, see Jiri Valenta, "Soviet Decision-Making on the Intervention in Angola," in David Albright, ed., *Communism in Africa* (Bloomington: Indiana University Press, 1976), pp. 57–71; and Peter Vanneman and W. Martin James, III, "Soviet Intervention in Angola: Intentions and Implications," *Strategic Review* (summer 1976), pp. 127–36.
6. *Foreign Report*, June 9, 1988, p. 3; the 1987 figure is from the *Washington Post*, May 5, 1987, p. 6.
7. *Washington Post*, November 12, 1987, p. A33; the *Christian Science Monitor*, October 6, 1987, p. 4, quotes the Angolan. Francis Fukuyama notes that there were Soviet advisers at the battalion level in 1985 ("Gorbachev and the Third World," *Foreign Affairs* [spring 1986]: 722). *Jane's Defense Weekly*, October 24, 1987, estimates as high as 70–90 "advisers" per battalion in 1987.
8. On early Soviet interest in Angola, see V. Sidenko, "The Last African Colonies: Angola," *New Times* (Moscow, December 1960), p. 20; and "Africa Today: The Soviet View," *Mizan Newsletter* (London, April 1962), p. 3.
9. On early KGB activities in Angola, see *Ghana White Paper* (Accra, Ghana, 1966). The KGB now has eleven known operatives in neighboring Zambia and three in neighboring Zaire. John Marcum alludes to KGB effectiveness just before independence in "The Lessons of Angola," *Foreign Affairs* (April 1976): 414; see also Roger Morris, "The Proxy of War in Angola: Pathology of a Blunder," *New Republic*, January 31, 1976, p. 21. On MPLA contacts with the Portuguese and Angolan Communist Parties, see Richard Gibson, *African Liberation Movements* (London: Oxford University Press, 1971), pp. 211–12.
10. The State Department figure is cited in Bruce D. Porter, *The USSR in Third World Conflicts* (Cambridge, Eng.: Cambridge University Press, 1984), p. 156.

11. *Daily Telegraph* (London), April 11, 1975, pp. 1, 8.
12. Arkady N. Shevchenko, *Breaking with Moscow* (New York: Alfred Knopf, 1985), p. 273.
13. Porter, *Third World Conflicts*, p. 156.
14. On early Soviet arms deliveries, see Senate Committee on Foreign Relations, Angola hearings, 94th Cong., 2d sess., 1976, p. 184.
15. *Granma Weekly Review*, May 2, 1976, p. 1; *Washington Post*, January 12, 1977, p. 3.
16. The remaining details of this initial intervention are drawn from Porter, *Third World Conflicts*, p. 156.
17. *Washington Post*, January 5, 1984, p. 1.
18. *Economist*, March 30, 1985, p. 21; the remaining details are from Peter Vanneman, "The USSR and Angola," *Strategic Review* (June 1985): 283.
19. *Christian Science Monitor*, January 19, 1984, p. 10.
20. *Economist*, July 30, 1983, p. 39.
21. *Sunday Times* (London), September 24, 1985, p. 7.
22. *Jane's Defense Weekly*, October 12, 1985, p. 776; and confidential interviews.
23. *Washington Post*, in *AFP Press Clips*, October 11, 1985, p. 5.
24. *Washington Post*, November 12, 1987, p. A33. *Christian Science Monitor*, October 6, 1987, p. 2, quotes the Angolan. *Jane's Defense Weekly*, October 24, 1987, p. 950, gives the 70–90 figure from an unidentified source.
25. *Washington Post*, November 12, 1987, p. A33.
26. For the Angolan claim, see *Africa Confidential*, October 7, 1987, p. 1; for the South African claim, see *Jane's Defense Weekly*, November 28, 1987, p. 1241.
27. William Claiborne of the *Washington Post* personally saw Cuban and Soviet pilots getting into heavily armed MIG-23 fighters (*Washington Post*, October 4, 1987, in *AFP Press Clips*, October 9, 1987, p. 8).
28. *Jane's Defense Weekly*, October 24, 1987, p. 950; *Washington Post*, November 2, 1987, p. A17.
29. *Jane's Defense Weekly*, October 24, 1987, p. 950.
30. *Jane's Defense Weekly*, November 14, 1987, p. 2; *Africa Confidential*, October 7, 1987, p. 1; and *Jane's Defense Weekly*, November 28, 1987, p. 1241.
31. *Jane's Defense Weekly*, October 24, 1987, p. 950.
32. Ibid.
33. Ibid.
34. *Africa Confidential*, November 18, 1987, p. 2; *Africa Confidential*, October 7, 1987, p. 1; and *Jane's Defense Weekly*, November 28, 1987, p. 1241.
35. *New York Times*, December 15, 1987, in *AFP Press Clips*, December 18, 1987, p. 15.
36. *New York Times*, December 16, 1987, in *AFP Press Clips*, December 18, 1987, p. 6.

37. *Pravda*, January 13, 1984, p. 1.
38. AIM press release (Mozambican government) quoted in *Washington Post*, December 6, 1987, p. A47.
39. *Washington Post*, December 6, 1987, p. A47.
40. *Africa Confidential*, February 5, 1988, p. 2.
41. *New York Times*, December 21, 1987, p. 6.
42. Ibid.
43. AIM press release (Mozambican government) quoted in *Washington Post*, December 6, 1987, p. A47; *Christian Science Monitor*, March 6, 1988, in *AFP Press Clips*, March 11, 1988, p. 6.
44. *New York Times*, December 16, 1987, in *AFP Press Clips*, December 18, 1987, p. 6.
45. *New York Times*, May 31, 1988, in *AFP Press Clips*, June 3, 1988, p. 5.
46. *Baltimore Sun*, April 25, 1988, in *AFP Press Clips*, May 6, 1988, p. 3.
47. *Jane's Defense Weekly*, April 30, 1988, p. 833.
48. *New York Times*, December 21, 1987, p. 6.
49. *New York Times*, May 18, 1988, in *AFP Press Clips*, May 20, 1988, p. 4.
50. *New York Times*, December 21, 1987, p. 6.
51. *New York Times*, April 20, 1988, in *AFP Press Clips*, April 22, 1988, p. 4; *Africa Confidential*, April 2, 1988, p. 182.
52. *Foreign Report*, April 13, 1989, p. 4.

Chapter 6

1. Thomas Henriksen, "Lusophone Africa: Angola, Mozambique, and Guinea-Bissau," in Peter Duignan and Robert Jackson, eds., *Politics and Government in African States, 1960–1985* (Stanford: Hoover Institution Press, 1986), p. 387.
2. Karen L. Puschel, "The USSR and Lusophone Africa," in *The USSR and Marxist Revolutions in the Third World"* (Washington: Kennan Institute of Woodrow Wilson Center, 1987), p. 34.
3. Radio Maputo, May 22, 1985, *FBIS*, May 28, 1986; Richard F. Staar, ed., *1987 Yearbook of Communist Affairs* (Stanford: Hoover Institution Press, 1987), p. xxx; Moscow Radio (in Russian), *FBIS-Sov*, May 17, 1985, p. C2.
4. L. Adele Jinadu, "Soviet Influence on Afro-Marxist Regimes," in Edmond Keller and Donald Rothchild, eds., *Afro-Marxist Regimes: Ideology and Public Policy* (Boulder, Colo.: Lynne Rienner Publishers, 1987), p. 243.
5. BBC "Review of World Events," ME/6843/ii, October 2, 1981.
6. *New Times* (Moscow), no. 10 (March 1983): 26–28.
7. *Foreign Report*, January 8, 1987, p. 6.
8. Gillian Gunn, "Cuba and Mozambique," *Center for Strategic and International Studies (CSIS) Africa Notes*, December 28, 1987, p. 8.

9. Jinadu, "Afro-Marxist Regimes," p. 244.
10. Gunn, "Cuba and Mozambique," p. 8.
11. Peter Vanneman and W. Martin James, III, *Soviet Foreign Policy in Southern Africa: Problems and Prospects* (Pretoria: Africa Institute of Southern Africa, 1982), p. 46.
12. Henriksen, "Lusophone Africa," pp. 386–92, outlines the future of Soviet foreign economic policy, particularly the state farms; see also Helen Kitchen, ed., *Angola, Mozambique and the West* (New York: Praeger, 1987), especially chapters 6, 7, 8.
13. Henriksen, "Lusophone Africa," p. 389; and Crawford Young, *Ideology and Development in Africa*, (New Haven, Conn.: Yale University Press, 1982), p. 95.
14. Moscow Radio (in Russian), *FBIS-Sov*, April 23, 1985; Moscow Radio (in Russian), *FBIS-Middle East and Africa (MEA)*, 87–090, May 4, 1987; and Jinadu, "Afro-Marxist Regimes," p. 246.
15. *Soviet Foreign Trade Statistics* (in English) (Moscow: Progress Publishers, 1985), pp. 10–24.
16. Peter Vanneman, "Soviet Foreign Economic Policy in the Third World: The Case of Mozambique After Nkomati," *Strategic Review* (December 1984): 2–4.
17. Ibid.
18. Radio Maputo, May 22, 1985, *FBIS*, May 28, 1986; Richard F. Staar, ed., *1987 Yearbook of Communist Affairs* (Stanford: Hoover Institution Press, 1987), p. xxx; Moscow Radio (in Russian), *FBIS-Sov*, May 17, 1985, p. C2.
19. Moscow Radio (in Russian), *FBIS-Sov*, May 17, 1985, p. C2; and Vanneman, "Soviet Foreign Economic Policy," pp. 2–4.
20. Moscow Radio (in English), *FBIS-MEA*, May 28, 1986.
21. BBC "Review of World Events," ME/8324/13, July 30, 1986.
22. *Congressional Record*, Senate S4807, May 1, 1987; and *FBIS-MEA*, May 11, 1987.
23. *FBIS-MEA*, May 11, 1987.

Chapter 7

1. *Pravda*, October 26, 1985, contains the draft party program adopted at the 27th CPSU Congress in March 1986.
2. L. H. Gann and Peter Duignan, *Africa South of the Sahara: The Challenge to Western Security* (Stanford: Hoover Institution Press, 1981), p. 95.
3. Richard Lowenthal, *Model or Ally: The Communist Powers and the Developing Countries* (Oxford: Oxford University Press, 1977), pp. 359–76.
4. Richard E. Bissell, "Union of Soviet Socialist Republics," in Thomas H. Henriksen, ed., *Communist Powers and Sub-Saharan Africa* (Stanford: Hoover Institution Press, 1981), p. 18.

5. Robert H. Jackson, "Conclusion," in Peter Duignan and Robert H. Jackson, eds., *Politics and Government in African States: 1960–1985* (Stanford: Hoover Institution Press, 1986), p. 422.
6. Estimates based on interviews with Western intelligence, cited in *Backgrounder*, July 21, 1986, p. 6.
7. Bissell, "Union of Soviet Socialist Republics," p. 16.
8. *World Military Expenditures, 1985*, (Washington, D.C.: Heritage Foundation, August 1985), p. 132.
9. *Pravda*, March 15, 1984; *Izvestia*, October 4, 1984; *FBIS-USSR*, May 1, 1981, p. J2.
10. *Jane's Defense Weekly*, November 28, 1987, p. 1243.
11. *FBIS-Sov*, May 19, 1987, p. 96.
12. L. H. Gann and Peter Duignan, "Namibia, Botswana, Lesotho, and Swaziland," in Duignan and Jackson, *African States*, p. 366.
13. BBC "Review of World Events," SU/8574, May 22, 1987.
14. BBC "Review of World Events," SU/W/433/A, May 29, 1987.
15. Estimates based on interviews with Western intelligence, cited in *Backgrounder*, July 21, 1986, p. 6.
16. Richard Cornwell, "Botswana," *Bulletin of the Africa Institute* 22, no. 4 (1982): 26–27.
17. *World Military Expenditures, 1985*, p. 132.
18. Peter Vanneman and W. Martin James, III, *Soviet Foreign Policy in Southern Africa: Problems and Prospects* (Pretoria: Africa Institute of South Africa, 1982), p. 49.
19. Maseru Domestic Service, August 22, 1984, trans. in *FBIS-MEA*, June 15, 1984, p. 62.
20. *Izvestia*, August 7, 1984, p. 3.
21. *Pravda*, September 6, 1984.
22. *Backgrounder*, July 21, 1986, p. 5; *Economist*, January 25, 1986, p. 32.
23. *Africa Confidential*, March 4, 1988, p. 6, identifies the ministers as Michael Sefali, Minister for Planning, and Khalaki Sello, Minister for Law.
24. For an excellent summary of the insurgency, see Thomas Henriksen, *The Struggle for Zimbabwe: Battle in the Bush* (London: Faber, 1981).
25. Zimbabwe's economic prosperity is threatened by the ruling party's call for more state intervention and by the mushrooming size of the state bureaucracy, which grew from 49,000 civil servants in 1979 to 86,000 in 1984. See L. H. Gann, "Malawi, Zambia, and Zimbabwe," in Duignan and Jackson, *African States*, pp. 179, 183. On the Soviet planes, see *Washington Post*, April 17, 1987, p. 2.
26. Kurt Campbell, *Southern Africa in Soviet Foreign Policy*, Adelphi Paper no. 227 (winter 1987/88): 20–21.
27. Gann, "Malawi, Zambia, and Zimbabwe," p. 183.

28. Campbell, *Southern Africa*, p. 21.
29. Ibid., p. 20.
30. *Pravda*, September 15, 1983.
31. *Pravda*, August 8, 1984.
32. On Mugabe's visit, see *FBIS-Sov*, December 5, 1985, pp. J1–8, December 4, 1985, pp. J1–7, and December 3, 1985, pp. J6.
33. *Backgrounder*, July 21, 1986, p. 8.
34. Ibid.
35. *Washington Post*, April 17, 1987, p. 2. It also appeared in the *Observer* (London) and the *Daily Telegraph* (London). For a detailed South African version of this episode, see A. Wildshut, "Will Zimbabwe Soon Have Mig-29s?" *Soviet Review*, July–August 1982, pp. 1–5. On Jordan's MIG-29 deal and the arrival of Soviet trainers, see *Jane's Defense Weekly*, February 6, 1988, p. 200.
36. Crawford Young, "Zaire and Cameroon," in Duignan and Jackson, *African States*, pp. 120–62, provides a succinct account of Zaire's domestic situation.
37. *Pravda*, October 26, 1985.
38. *Africa Confidential*, May 27, 1988, p. 1.
39. Dan Heldman, *The USSR and Africa: Foreign Policy Under Khrushchev* (New York: Praeger, 1981). On this era see Christopher Stevens, *The Soviet Union and Black Africa* (London: Macmillan, 1976); and Helen Cohn, *Soviet Policy Toward Black Africa: The Focus on National Integration* (New York: Praeger, 1971).
40. Young, "Zaire and Cameroon," p. 135.
41. Christopher Coker, *NATO, the Warsaw Pact and Africa* (London: Macmillan, 1984), p. 124.
42. Ibid., p. 198.
43. *The Observer* (London), May 21, 1978, p. 7.
44. Peter Vanneman, "Soviet Intervention in Zaire: Shaba II" (Paper delivered to Foreign Affairs Conference, Hamburg, Germany, 1978), p. 3.
45. *Christian Science Monitor*, January 16, 1979, p. 3, and confidential interview with an eyewitness.
46. See Peter Vanneman, *The Supreme Soviet: Politics and the Legislative Process in the Soviet Political System* (Durham, N.C.: Duke University Press, 1977), pp. 172–75; and David Albright, *Soviet Policy Toward Africa Revisited* (Washington: *Center for Strategic and International Studies*, 1987), pp. 31–32.
47. Albright, *Soviet Policy*, pp. 31–32.
48. BBC "Review of World Events," ME/8622/B, July 17, 1987.

Chapter 8

1. Vernon Aspaturian, "Gorbachev's New Political Thinking and the Angolan Conflict" (Paper delivered at the Fourth International Conference, Gorbachev's New Thinking and Soviet/Cuban Strategy in Africa, University of Miami, Institute of Soviet and East European Studies, December 21, 1988), stresses the importance of American initiatives.
2. Michael Armacost, undersecretary of state, "Regional Issues and U.S.-Soviet Relations," Current Policy Paper, no. 1089, p. 5; *New York Times*, October 30, 1988, p. 6.
3. *Washington Times*, May 30, 1988, p. A8.
4. *FBIS-Africa* 88-196, October 11, 1988, pp. 16, 17.
5. *New York Times*, October 30, 1988, p. 6; *New York Times*, November 2, 1988, p. 27.
6. *Jane's Defense Weekly*, November 26, 1988, p. 1322.
7. *New York Times*, December 5, 1988, p. 8.
8. Ibid.
9. *New York Times*, October 2, 1988, p. 3.
10. *Washington Post*, October 9, 1988, in *AFP Press Clips*, October 14, 1988, p. 4.
11. Peter Vanneman, "The USSR and the Angolan Conflict" (Paper delivered at the Fourth International Conference, Gorbachev's New Thinking and Soviet/Cuban Strategy in Africa, University of Miami, Institute of Soviet and East European Studies, December 21, 1988), p. 24.
12. Peter Vanneman and W. Martin James, III, *Soviet Foreign Policy in Southern Africa: Problems and Prospects* (Pretoria: Africa Institute of South Africa, 1982), pp. 43–45, notes the escalating naval presence in the late 1970s and early 1980s.
13. Ibid., p. 43.
14. Soviet warships were used against anti-MPLA forces in the Angolan civil war. See *Peking Review*, September 5, 1975, p. 22. Also, the Soviets bombarded the coastal cities of Massawa and Assab in the 1978 Ethiopian intervention, according to the *New York Times*, May 17, 1978, p. 1, and the *Christian Science Monitor*, January 30, 1978, p. 1.
15. Vanneman and James, *Soviet Foreign Policy*, pp. 43–45.
16. Ibid.
17. Richard Bissell, "The Union of Soviet Socialist Republics," in Thomas H. Henriksen, ed., *Communist Powers and Sub-Saharan Africa* (Stanford: Hoover Institution Press, 1981), p. 8.
18. Christopher Coker, *NATO, the Warsaw Pact and Africa*, (London: Macmillan, 1984), p. 99, describes the following deployments.
19. Adam Ulam, *Dangerous Relations: The Soviet Union in World Politics, 1970–1982* (Oxford: Oxford University Press, 1983), pp. 134–35.

20. *Sunday Times* (London), June 19, 1988, p. 4.
21. Peter Vanneman and Martin James, "Soviet Intervention in Angola: Intentions and Implications," *Strategic Review* (summer 1976), pp. 97–108, also reprinted in *The International Environment: Africa* (Norfolk, Va.: U.S. Armed Forces Staff College), for instructional use only, pp. 134–45.
22. *New York Times*, July 20, 1988, p. 2, citing "American officials."
23. Francis Fukuyama, "Gorbachev and the Third World," *Foreign Affairs* (spring 1986): 724.
24. *Jane's Defense Weekly*, October 24, 1987, p. 950, states that there were 70–90 Soviet "advisers" with some Angolan battalions.
25. *Africa Confidential*, May 27, 1988, p. 8.
26. The author has seen notebooks of Angolan officers trained by the Soviets that contain evidence of instruction about chemical warfare.
27. David Martin and Phyllis Johnson, *The Struggle for Zimbabwe: The Chimurenga War* (London: Faber, 1981), pp. 305–9, describes this episode.
28. Gillian Gunn, "Cuba and Angola," *CSIS Africa Notes*, March 31, 1987, pp. 1–8.
29. *New York Times*, July 28, 1988, p. 5. In June 1984 Castro was the only member head of state not to attend the CMEA meeting in Moscow, prompting speculation about friction, but this ultimately amounted to nothing.
30. Boris Asoyan, Soviet ambassador to Lesotho, "A Soviet Diplomat's View of South Africa," *South Africa Foundation Review* (June 1988): 7.
31. Coker, *NATO*, p. 187.
32. Kuznetsov is quoted by Arkady Shevchenko, *Breaking with Moscow* (New York: Knopf, 1985), p. 273.
33. Augustino Neto, "Let the Struggle Continue," *Afriscope* (December 1975): 62.
34. *FBIS/MEA*, July 21, 1982, p. 5.; *Christian Science Monitor*, May 4, 1987, in *AFP Press Clips*, May 6, 1987, p. 7.
35. *New York Times*, December 11, 1987, in *AFP Press Clips*, December 18, 1987, p. 7.
36. Ibid., quoting Cuban defectors to the U.S.
37. See Martin and Johnson, *Zimbabwe*, pp. 305–9.
38. Klaus Lange, "The Current Soviet View of Southern and South Africa," *Soviet Review*, March-April, 1988, p. 18.
39. Richard Staar, "Foreword," in Thomas H. Henriksen, ed., *Communist Powers and Sub-Saharan Africa* (Stanford: Hoover Institution Press, 1981), p. ix. "All the contributors are in agreement that the subcontinent's chronic instability due to increasing conflict and the presence of valuable resources suggests growing opportunities for the communist-ruled states of the world."

Chapter 9

1. See Louis George Sarris, "Soviet Military Policy and Arms Activities in Sub-Saharan Africa," in W. Foltz and H. Bienen eds., *Arms and the African: Military Influences on Africa's International Relations* (New Haven, Conn.: Yale University Press, 1985), pp. 29–59; and Christopher Coker, *NATO, The Warsaw Pact and Africa,* (London: Macmillan, 1984), pp. 1–237.
2. L. H. Gann and Peter Duignan, *Africa South of the Sahara: The Challenge to Western Security* (Stanford: Hoover Institution Press, 1981), pp. 74, 75.
3. John P. Hardt, "Soviet Non-Fuel Minerals Policy: The Global Context," *Journal of Resource Management and Technology* 12, no. 1 (January 1983): 57–62.
4. James A. Miller, *Strategic Minerals and the West* (Washington, D.C.: American African Affairs Association, 1980), p. 58; James E. Sinclair and Robert Parker, *The Strategic Metals War* (New York: Arlington House, 1983), especially pp. 66–77; U.S. Congress, Office of Technology Assessment, *Strategic Minerals* (Washington, D.C.: GPO, 1985), p. 409.
5. Coker, *NATO*, p. 187.
6. Christopher Coker, "Soviet Bloc Economic Interests in Southern Africa," *Soviet Revue,* March–April 1988, p. 5.
7. John Harrison, "The Soviet International Banking System" (Master's thesis, University of Arkansas, 1976).
8. Kurt Campbell, *Soviet Policy Towards South Africa* (New York: St. Martins, 1986), especially p. 94.
9. The company is DeBeers. Coker, "Soviet Bloc," p. 9, asserts that "in the mid-1970s, its payments to the Soviet Union represented the USSR's largest source of hard currency after the sale of gold and petroleum."
10. Confidential interview with eyewitness.
11. For analyses of these schools of thought, see Peter Vanneman and W. Martin James, III, "The Rise of Opinion Groups in the Soviet African Policy Process," *Journal of Contemporary African Studies* 2, no. 2 (1983): 15–33; and David Albright, "Soviet Policy Toward Africa Revisited," *CSIS Africa Notes,* 1987, pp. 19–28.
12. An insightful appreciation of the role of ethnicity is found in V. Chirkin, "Strany sotsialisticheskoi orientatsii: razvitie revoliutsionnykh partii," *Aziia i Afrika segodniia* (August 1981).
13. *New York Times,* March 1984, p. 11.
14. For an excellent overview of Soviet nationalities policy, see Donald W. Treadgold, "Nationalism in the USSR and Its Implications for the World," in Robert Conquest, ed., *The Last Empire: Nationality and the Soviet Future* (Stanford: Hoover Institution Press, 1986), p. 381.
15. Zhores Medvedev, *Gorbachev* (Ontario: Norton, 1986), p. 23, "Stavropol was built in 1777–78 as a fortress to secure the new frontiers of the Russian Empire from the mostly Moslem inhabitants of the North Caucasus." See also pages 32

and 33, which discuss Gorbachev's role in resettling Moslems displaced by Stalin during the war.
16. Teresa Rakowska-Harmstone, "Soviet Central Asia: A Model of Non-Capitalist Development for the Third World," in Yaacov Ro'i, ed., *The USSR and the Muslim World* (London: Allen & Unwin, 1985), p. 181.
17. Peter Manchka, *V avangarde revoliutsionno-osvoboditel'noi bor'by v Afrike* (Moscow: Politizdat, 1975), p. 46. A. Gromyko, director of the Africa Institute, refutes Manchka in "Socialist Orientation in Africa," in *The Ideology of African Revolutionary Democracy* (Moscow: USSR Academy of Sciences, 1984), pp. 16–17.
18. Gleb Starushenko, "Problems of Struggle Against Racism, Apartheid, Colonialism in South Africa" (Report presented to the Second Soviet-African Conference, For Peace, Cooperation and Social Progress, Moscow, June 24–26, 1986), Moscow: USSR Academy of Sciences, Africa Institute, 1986.
19. *London Times,* February 17, 1950, p. 3; and Awoonor-Renner, *West African Soviet Union* (London: Samarkand Publishers, 1946), pp. 16–23.
20. *New York Times Magazine,* December 6, 1987, p. 102.
21. Richard Staar, *USSR Foreign Policies After Détente,* rev. ed. (Stanford: Hoover Institution Press, 1987), pp. 79–80.
22. *Washington Post,* October 9, 1988, in *AFP Press Clips,* October 14, 1988, p. 4.
23. Thomas H. Henriksen, *Communist Powers and Sub-Saharan Africa* (Stanford: Hoover Institution Press, 1981), pp. 1–126.
24. Peter Vanneman and W. Martin James, III, *Soviet Foreign Policy in Southern Africa: Problems and Prospects* (Pretoria: Africa Institute of South Africa, 1982), pp. 11–12.
25. Elisaveta Kandyba-Foxcroft, *Russia and the Anglo-Boer War: 1899–1902* (Roodepoort, South Africa: Cum Books, 1981), pp. 1–407.
26. Richard Bissell, "The Union of Soviet Socialist Republics," in Henriksen, *Sub-Saharan Africa,* p. 3.
27. Edward Wilson, *Russia and Black Africa Before World War II* (New York: Holmes and Meier, 1974), p. 295.
28. Much has been made about the globalists and the regionalists, allegedly two schools of thought in America, regarding Soviet intentions and motivations in the region. In fact, Soviet strategy has displayed a singular continuity since Brezhnev's reassessment in 1969. Dividing analysts into regionalists and globalists is a false dichotomy belied by the strategic continuity reflected in Soviet behavior. For a synopsis of this, see Donald Jordan, *Changing American Assessments of the Soviet Threat in Sub-Saharan Africa: 1975–1985* (Lanham, Md.: University of America Press, 1987), pp. 1–97.
29. *Foreign Report,* June 9, 1988, p. 4, gives the NATO figure.
30. Coker, "Soviet Bloc," p. 4.
31. Tony Hodges, *Angola to the 1990s: The Potential for Recovery* (London: Economist, 1987), pp. 1–28.

32. Wilson, *Russia and Black Africa*, p. 173.
33. V. I. Lenin Speech to the Third Comintern Congress, July 5, 1921, in International Press Correspondence 8, no. 17, p. 232.
34. See S. Neil MacFarlane, *Superpower Rivalry and Third World Radicalism: The Idea of National Liberation* (Baltimore: Johns Hopkins University Press, 1985), p. 185. "The basic outlines of Soviet doctrine in the Third World have remained quite stable since the death of Stalin. What variation occurs tends to be cyclical, and can be accounted for largely in terms of political exigency and shifts in Soviet attitudes between optimism and pessimism with regard to their own development, the international correlation of forces, and the course of events in the Third World."
35. Vernon Aspaturian, "Gorbachev's New Political Thinking and the Angolan Conflict" (Paper delivered at Fourth International Conference, Gorbachev's New Thinking and Soviet/Cuban Strategy in Africa, University of Miami, Institute of Soviet and East European Studies, December 21, 1988).
36. In March 1989, Deputy Foreign Minister Anatoly Adamishin praised Soviet coercive diplomacy in Angola for changes inside South Africa: "The main causes for changes were South Africa's defeat at the battle of Cuito Cuanavale" (*Soviet Review*, May–June 1989, p. 35).

SELECTED BIBLIOGRAPHY

Albright, David E. *Soviet Policy Toward Africa Revisited.* Significant Issues Series, vol. 9, no. 6. Washington, D.C.: The Center for Strategic and International Studies, 1987.

Anderson, Annelise, and Bark, Dennis L., eds. *Thinking About America: The United States in the 1990s.* Stanford: Hoover Institution Press, 1988.

Brown, Archie, and Kaser, Michael, eds. *Soviet Policy for the 1980s.* Oxford: Macmillan Press, 1982.

Campbell, Kurt M. *Soviet Policy Towards South Africa.* New York: St. Martin's Press, 1986.

——. *Southern Africa in Soviet Foreign Policy.* Adelphi Paper 227. London: International Institute for Strategic Studies, Winter 1987/88.

Clough, Michael, ed. *Reassessing the Soviet Challenge in Africa.* Policy Papers in International Affairs; Institute of International Studes. Berkeley: University of California, 1986.

Cohn, Helen Desfosses. *Soviet Policy Toward Black Africa: The Focus on National Integration.* New York: Praeger Publishers, 1971.

Coker, Christopher. *NATO, the Warsaw Pact and Africa.* London: Macmillan Press, 1984.

Davis, Stephen M. *Apartheid's Rebels: Inside South Africa's Hidden War.* New Haven, Conn.: Yale University Press, 1987.

de Haas, M. *Sojetbeleid ten aanzien van Zuidelijk Afrika.* Utrecht, the Netherlands: B. V. Uitgeverij, 1988.

Duignan, Peter, and Jackson, Robert H. *Politics and Government in African States: 1960–1985.* Stanford: Hoover Institution Press, 1986.

du Pisani, Andre. *SWA/Namibia: The Politics of Continuity and Change.* Johannesburg: Jonathan Ball Publishers, 1986.

Falk, Pamela S. *Cuban Foreign Policy.* Lexington, Mass.: Lexington Books, 1986.

Foltz, William J., and Bienen, Henry S., eds. *Arms and the African: Military Influences on Africa's International Relations.* New Haven, Conn.: Yale University Press, 1985.

Foreign Policy Research Institute. *Soviet Activities in Sub-Saharan Africa*. Final Report. Philadelphia, Pa.: Foreign Policy Research Institute, 1988.

Foxcroft, Elisaveta Kandyba. *Russia and the Anglo-Boer War: 1899–1902*. Roodepoort, South Africa: Cum Books, 1981.

Friedman, Steven, and Narsov, Monty. *A New Mood in Moscow: Soviet Attitudes to South Africa*. Johannesburg: South African Institute of Race Relations, 1989.

Gann, Lewis H., and Duignan, Peter. *Why South Africa Will Survive*. Cape Town: Tafelberg Publishers, 1981.

———. *Africa Between East and West*. Cape Town: Tafelberg Publishers, 1983.

Gann, Lewis H., and Henriksen, Thomas H. *The Struggle for Zimbabwe: Battle in the Bush*. New York: Praeger Publishers, 1981.

Gavshon, Arthur. *Crisis in Africa: Battleground of East and West*. New York: Penguin Books, 1981.

Gibson, Richard. *African Liberation Movements: Contemporary Struggle Against White Minority Rule*. Oxford: Oxford University Press, 1971.

Grundy, Kenneth W. *Guerrilla Struggle in Africa: An Analysis and Preview*. New York: Grossman Publishers, 1971.

Heldman, Dan C. *The USSR and Africa: Foreign Policy Under Khrushchev*. New York: Praeger Publishers, 1981.

Henriksen, Thomas H., ed. *Communist Powers and Sub-Saharan Africa*. Stanford: Hoover Institution Press, 1981.

Hough, Jerry F. *The Struggle for the Third World: Soviet Debates and American Options*. Washington, D.C.: Brookings Institution, 1986.

Jordan, Donald. *Changing American Assessments of the Soviet Threat in Sub-Saharan Africa: 1975–1985*. Lanham, Md.: University Press of America, 1987.

Kanet, Roger E., ed. *Soviet Foreign Policy in the 1980s*. New York: Praeger Publishers, 1982.

Katz, Mark N. *The Third World in Soviet Military Thought*. Baltimore: Johns Hopkins University Press, 1982.

Keller, Edmond J., and Rothchild, Donald, eds. *Afro-Marxist Regimes: Ideology and Public Policy*. Boulder, Colo.: Lynne Rienner Publishers, 1987.

Kempton, Daniel R. *Soviet Strategy Toward Southern Africa: The National Liberation Movement Connection*. New York: Praeger Publishers, 1989.

Kennan Institute for Advanced Russian Studies, Woodrow Wilson International Center for Scholars. *The USSR and Marxist Revolutions in the Third World*. Washington, D.C.: Woodrow Wilson International Center for Scholars, 1987.

Kitchen, Helen, ed. *Angola, Mozambique, and the West*. The Washington Papers 130, The Center for Strategic and International Studies. New York: Praeger Publishers, 1987.

Kolodziej, Edward A., and Kanet, Roger E. *The Limits of Soviet Power in the Developing World*. Baltimore: Johns Hopkins University Press, 1989.

Korbonski, Andrzej, and Fukuyama, Francis, eds. *The Soviet Union and the Third World: The Last Three Decades.* Ithaca, N.Y.: Cornell University Press, 1987.

Kühne, Winrich. *Die Politik der Sowjetunion in Afrika.* Baden-Baden: Nomos Verlagsgeseuschuft, 1983.

Legum, Colin; Zartman, I. William; Langdon, Steven; and Mytelka, Lynn K. *Africa in the 1980s: A Continent in Crisis.* 1980s Project, Council on Foreign Relations. New York: McGraw-Hill, 1979.

MacFarlane, S. Neil. *Superpower Rivalry and Third World Radicalism: The Idea of National Liberation.* Baltimore: Johns Hopkins University Press, 1985.

Martin, David, and Johnson, Phyllis. *The Struggle for Zimbabwe: The Chimurenga War.* London: Faber and Faber, 1981.

Menon, Rajan. *Soviet Power and the Third World.* New Haven, Conn.: Yale University Press, 1986.

Morison, David. *The USSR and Africa.* London: Oxford University Press, 1964.

Nation, R. Craig, and Kauppi, Mark V., eds. *The Soviet Impact in Africa.* Lexington, Mass.: Lexington Books, 1984.

Nel, Philip. *Die USSR en Suidelike Afrika: Aspekte van Beleid.* Stellenbosch, South Africa: University of Stellenbosch, 1987.

Nielsen, Waldemar A. *The Great Powers and Africa.* New York: Praeger Publishers, 1969.

Norval, Morgan. *Red Star Over Southern Africa.* Washington, D.C.: Selous Foundation Press, 1988.

Ogunbadejo, Oye. *The International Politics of Africa's Strategic Minerals.* London: Frances Pinter, 1985.

Payne, Richard J. *Opportunities and Dangers of Soviet-Cuban Expansion: Toward a Pragmatic U.S. Policy.* Albany: State University of New York Press, 1988.

Pike, Henry R. *A History of Communism in South Africa.* Germiston, South Africa: Christian Mission International of South Africa, 1985.

Porter, Bruce D. *The USSR in Third World Conflicts: Soviet Arms and Diplomacy in Local Wars 1945–1980.* Cambridge, Eng.: Cambridge University Press, 1984.

Rotberg, Robert I., ed. *Namibia: Political and Economic Prospects.* Cape Town: David Philip, 1983.

Rothenberg, Morris. *The USSR and Africa: New Dimensions of Soviet Global Power.* Monographs in International Affairs. Washington, D.C.: Advanced International Studies Institute, 1980.

Rubinstein, Alvin Z. *Moscow's Third World Strategy.* Princeton, N.J.: Princeton University Press, 1989.

———. *Soviet Foreign Policy Since World War II: Imperial and Global.* 3rd ed. Glenview, Ill.: Scott, Foresman and Company, 1989.

Saivetz, Carol R., and Woodby, Sylvia. *Soviet-Third World Relations.* Boulder, Colo.: Westview Press, 1985.

Shultz, Richard H., and Godson, Roy. *Dezinformatsia: Active Measures in Soviet Strategy*. Washington, D.C.: Pergamon-Brassey's, 1984.

Staar, Richard F., ed. *Public Diplomacy: USA Versus USSR*. Stanford: Hoover Institution Press, 1986.

———. *USSR Foreign Policies After Détente*. Rev. ed. Stanford: Hoover Institution Press, 1987.

Stevens, Christopher. *The Soviet Union and Black Africa*. London: Macmillan Press, 1976.

U.S. Congress. Senate. Committee on the Judiciary. Subcommittee on Security and Terrorism. *The Role of the Soviet Union, Cuba, and East Germany in Fomenting Terrorism in Southern Africa—Volume 1*. Hearings. 97th Cong., 2nd sess., 1982. S. Rept. J-97-101.

U.S. Department of State. Bureau of Intelligence and Research. *Warsaw Pact Economic Aid Programs in Non-Communist LDCs: Holding Their Own in 1986*. Publication 9345. Rev. ed. August 1988.

Valkenier, Elizabeth Kridl. *The Soviet Union and the Third World: An Economic Bind*. New York: Praeger Publishers, 1983.

Vanneman, Peter, and James, W. Martin III. *Soviet Foreign Policy in Southern Africa: Problems and Prospects*. Pretoria: Africa Institute of South Africa, 1982.

van Rensburg, W. C. J., and Pretorius, D. A. *South Africa's Strategic Minerals: Pieces on a Continental Chess Board*. Johannesburg: Valiant Publishers, 1977.

Wilkinson, Paul. *Terrorism and the Liberal State*. London: Macmillan Press, 1977.

Wilson, Edward Thomas. *Russia and Black Africa Before World War II*. New York: Holmes and Meier Publishers, 1974.

Young, Crawford. *Ideology and Development in Africa*. New Haven, Conn.: Yale University Press, 1982.

INDEX

Adamishin, Anatoly L., 4, 23, 35, 83, 98
Afanasyev, Yuri, 19
Africa Institute of USSR Academy of Sciences, 3
African Communist, 9
African Countries Administration, Soviet, 4
African National Congress (ANC), 4, 5, 9, 15
   alliance with SACP, 25–26
   armed propaganda of, 14
   and armed struggle, 18–19
   in Botswana, 73
   ideological diversity of, 26–28
   internal conflict with SACP, 29
   leadership and USSR, 32–34
   leadership and violence, 28–29
   in Lesotho, 74
   Makiwane faction, 30
   military arm of, 21
   National Executive Council (NEC), 16
   Regional Political-Military Councils (RPMC), 29
   relations with China, 31
   Second Consultative Conference, 27, 28
   Soviet-Liberal talks, 18
   Soviet military and financial aid to, 19
   Soviet relations with, 13, 19, 25–26, 30, 34–35
   support for, 20
   white communists, 30
African-Soviet friction, 9
Aliyev, Geidar A., 1
ANC. *See* African National Congress
Andropov, Yuri V., 2
Angola, 45–57
   advanced weapons in, 51
   battles,
      Calueque Dam, 39–40, 43
      Lomba River, 51–53
      southern Africa's biggest, 55–56
   bush war in southern, 41–44
   confronting South Africa, 53–55
   Cuban troops and weapons in, 39–40
   escalation of conflict, 49
   Soviet coercive diplomacy in, 46–57
   Soviet Friendship Treaty, 46
   Soviet intervention in, 45
      Cuban presence, 48–49
      early involvement, 47–48
   Soviet military aid, 47
      equipment, 52, 54
      troops, 46
Angola-Namibia negotiations, 35
Anti-Apartheid Act of 1986, 25
Asoyan, Boris A., 3, 5, 6, 15, 18, 74
Aspaturian, Vernon, 3

Belayev, Igor A., 6
Bissell, Richard, 71, 86
Botha, P. W., 7, 27, 83
Botswana, democracy as constraint to Soviets, 72–73
Brezhnev Doctrine, 50
Broederbond, 7
Brutents, Karen A., 3, 11
Buthelezi, Gatsha, 31

Calueque Dam, battle of, 39–40, 43
Campbell, Kurt, 99
Carreira, Iko, 93
Castro, Fidel, 55
  and Cuban withdrawals from Angola, 83
  South Africa and, 38, 42, 60
Chemical warfare, Soviet use of, 90
Cherednik, Vladimir A., 5
Chernenko, Konstantin, 1
China
  increased involvement in Africa, 67
  Machel's visit to, 67
Chipenda, Daniel, 48, 93
Chissano, Joaquim, 60
CMEA, treaty for financial aid, 61
Coker, Christopher, 98, 105
Committee for Solidarity with Peoples of Asia and Africa, 5
Congress of South African Trade Unions (COSATU), 16
Coordinating Committee for Multilateral Export Controls (CoCom), 7
Council for Mutual Economic Assistance (CMEA), 98
Counterimperialism, 70
Cuito Cuanavale, attack on, 55

Deniability, 91
Disinformation and public diplomacy, Soviet, 5–8
Dlamini, Stephen, 33

Duignan, Peter, 70, 98
Dybenko, N. K., 1, 5

Embassy staffs, Soviet, expansion of, 6
Eminent Persons Group, 29

FNLA, U.S. aid to, 48
Foreign aid, and Russian nationalism, 11
Foreign Ministry, Soviet, southern African apparatus, 4–5
Frelimo, 58
  Soviet influence over, 59

Gann, L. H., 70, 98
Gavryushkin, Vladimir I., 5
Gebhardt, Dieter, 8
Gibson, Richard, 27
Gizenga, Antoine, 79
Glasnost, 9
Gogitze, Ivan A., 4
Goncharov, Leonard V., 6–7
Gorbachev, Mikhail S., 1–2, 11
  devious policies of, 22–24, 45
  flexible attitude of, 103
  policy in Mozambique, 58
  strategy for South Africa, 14–22
Gquiba, Fumanelike, 34
Gromyko, Anatoly A., 6, 7

Hani, Chris, 16, 21, 22, 23, 27, 33
Henriksen, Thomas, 11, 104

Ibragimov, Mirza I., 5
Inkatha, 101
Institute for Soviet Studies, 7
Institute of the USA and Canada, 3
Institute of World Economy and International Relations (IMEMO), 3

Index

International Department of CPSU
  southern African apparatus of, 3–4
Ivanovsky, Yevgeny, 59

Jackson, Robert H., 71
Jele, Josiah, 21
Jonathan, Lebua, 73–74

Kalinin, A. I., 5
Kapskiy, Eduard A., 4
Kasrils, Ronnie, 33
Katushev, Konstantin, 76
Kavango, SWAPO incursions in, 41
KGB, 7
  in Botswana, 73
  espionage and disinformation, 8–10
  in Zambia, 71
Khrushchev, Nikita S., 2
Kirilenko, Andrei V., 2
Klerk, F. W. de, 7
Kozlov, Alexei, 9
Kuznetsov, Vasily, 93

Lekanya, Justin, 74
Lesotho, South African power in, 73
Lithuli, Albert, 34
Lodge, Tom, 17
Loginov, Yuri, 9
Lowenthal, Richard, 70, 80
Low-risk globalism, Soviet, 12
Lukyanov, Anatoly, 24

Mabhida, Moses, 22
Machel, Samora, 1, 60, 61–62, 66
Maharaj, Mac, 33
Makana, Simon, 23
Make, Cassius, 21, 33
Makhele, Vincent, 74
Manchka, Petr, 4, 101–102
Mandela, Nelson, 32
  and expulsion of communists, 30
  release of and SACP, 24
  and violence, 28–29
Matabeleland, 76
Mbeki, Thabo, 23–24
Meli, Francis, 33
Midtsev, Vaniamin A., 4
Miroshkin, Oleg, 72
Moderate states of southern Africa, Soviet plans for, 80
Modise, Joe, 21, 32
Mompati, Ruth, 33
Mongale, Tony, 33
Mozambique, 58–69
  CMEA controversy, 65–66
  Cuban military advisers, 59
  Frelimo strength in, 67
  and International Monetary Fund, 67
  post-Nkomati foreign economic offensive, 63–65
  Soviet aid to, 61
  credits and grants, 62
  Soviet relations with, 68–69
  advisers, reduction in, 69
  economic constraints on, 66–68
  naval squadron in, 59
  rear guard in, 59–60
  trade, 63
Mozambique National Resistance, 20
MPLA. See Popular Movement for the Liberation of Angola (MPLA)
Mugabe, Robert, 75–77, 90–91, 93
Mushini, Alex, 23
Muzorewa, Abel, 90

Namibia, 37–44
  bush war in northern, 41–44
Namibia-Angola Accords, 22
National reconciliation, as Soviet strategy, 83
Naval and air facilities, access to, 96–97
Naval demonstrations, Soviet, 50
Necklacing, 28–29
Nel, Philip, 7

Neto, Augustino, 48, 92
Nkadimeng, John, 33
Nkobi, Thomas, 33
Nkomati Accords, 22, 64
Nkomo, Joshua, 75, 90, 92–93
Nkrumah, Kwame, 102
Nonaligned states, 70–80
Nujoma, Sam, 37, 42
Nyameko, R. S. *See* Simons, Ray
Nyerere, Julius, 92
Nzo, Alfred, 32–33

Ochoa Sanchez, Arnaldo, 39, 55–56
Okhela, 30
Operation Askari, 42, 46, 50, 86
Operation Hooper, 55
Operation Super, 41
Organization of African Unity (OAU), 19
Oriental Institute, 3
Ovamboland, SWAPO incursions in, 41

Pahad, Aziz, 33
Pan-African Congress (PAC), 22
  reason for, 30
Perestroika, 84
Petrov, Nicolai I., 5
Petruk, Boris I., 4
Pilaso, Mzwai, 33
Podgorny, Nikolai V., 2
Policy process, 1–12
Ponomarev, Boris, 48
Popular front strategy, Soviet, 15–16
Popular Movement for the Liberation of Angola (MPLA), 5, 49
  cadres to Moscow for military training, 48
  organization of, 47
Porter, Bruce, 48
Potekhin, Ivan I., 3
Pretoria-Washington axis, alleged, 30
Primakov, Yevgeny A., 3

Propaganda, Soviet, 100
Public diplomacy, Soviet, 11–12

Radio Moscow, 18
Reagan Doctrine, 84
Renamo, 68
Revolution, 27
Rodriguez, Carlos Rafael, 49
Russianization, 103
Russian national interest, 104

Sachs, Albie, 18
SACP. *See* South African Communist Party
Santos, President, 93
Savimbi, Jonas, 49, 82
Sechaba, 33
Shevardnadze, Eduard A., 2–3
Shevardnadze-Nujoma meeting, 37
Shubin, Vladimir I., 4
Sidebe, Glory Lephosha, 21
Sidenko, Viktor I., 4
Sigxashe, Sizakele, 33
Simons, Ray, 18
Sivimbi, 53
Slovo, Joe, 14–15, 21, 27, 30, 33
  and KGB, 21
  and violence, 28
Solodovnikov, Vasily G., 5, 18, 71
South Africa
  Soviet military aid and training, 19–22
  Soviet policy toward, 13, 49–53
  Soviet propaganda value of crisis over, 30
  terror in, 17
  white liberals, 17
South African Communist Party (SACP), 9, 24
  and armed struggle, 19
  penetration of unions, 16
  penetration of white opposition, 16–19

Politburo of, 14
two-stage revolutionary process, 15
South African Defense Force (SADF), 42
Southwest African People's Organization (SWAPO), 5, 9
  joint Cuban operations, 38–40
  opened Moscow mission, 37
  Soviet influence over, 42–44
Soviet Afro-Asian Solidarity Committee, 18
Soviet Committee for Afro-Asian Solidarity, 48, 74
Soviet-Mozambican Intergovernmental Commission for Economic and Technical Cooperation and Trade, 62, 64
Soviet Union
  African perceptions of, 103–104
  decision makers in, 2
  diplomacy of, 81–95
    "gunboat diplomacy," 85–87
  diplomatic relations with South Africa severed, 10
  economic aid to liberated countries, 2
  friction with ANC-SACP, 31
  global policy of, 104–107
  insensitivity, 72
  naval presence, reasons for, 85
  perceptions of Africa, 101–103
  policy advisers, 3
  proxy technique, 87–93
    air defense, 88
    assets and liabilities, 91
    Cuban proxy, 87–88
    specialized functions, 89
  strategy, 96–107
  and SWAPO, 37–44
Staar, Richard, 24
Starushenko, Gleb I., 6, 15, 102
Strategic minerals, 98–100
Stuart, James, 33
Suslov, Mikhail A., 2
SWAPO. *See* Southwest African People's Organization (SWAPO)

Tambo, Oliver, 19, 24, 32
  Christian beliefs, 34
  and expulsion of Communists, 30
  and violence, 28–29
  visit to China, 31
Tarabin, Yevgeny A., 84
Tloome, Dan, 30, 33
Toivo Ja Toivo, Herman, 42
Trinka, Edmund, 9
Tswete, Steve, 16–17, 33
Tutu, Desmond, 17

Ulam, Adam, 87
Ulyanovsky, Rostislav, 4, 6
Umkhonto, 23
Union for the Total Independence of Angola (UNITA), 10
  annual offensives against, 57
  insurgency, 50, 101
  U.S. support for, 56, 81
United Democratic Front (UDF), 16
Urnov, Andrei I., 4
Ustinov, Marshall, 60
Uvanovsky, Marshall, 60

Van Dunem, Pedro de Castro, 56
van Heerden, Neil, 83
Vasev, Vladilen I., 4, 83
Vasiliyev, Aleksandr I., 6

Wilson, Edward, 104
World Peace Council, 33

Yakalov, Yuri, 7
Yakovlev, Alexander N., 3, 11, 101
Yazov, Dmitri, 57
Yepishev, Alexei, 60
Yukalov, Yuri, 4

Zaire
  invaded by Angolans, 79
  Soviet coercive diplomacy in, 78–80
Zambia
  instability as Soviet opportunity, 71–72
  Soviet arms in, 71
ZANU, 91
ZAPU
  based in Zambia, 71
  Soviet support for, 78
Zimbabwe
  insecurity as Soviet opportunity, 75–78
  relations with U.S., 75
  Soviet disinformation in, 76
  Soviet weapons in, 76
Zimbabwe *Herald*, 10

About the Author

PETER VANNEMAN is a Senior Research Fellow at the J. William Fulbright Institute of International Relations and Professor of Political Science at the University of Arkansas. He has served as a consultant to the U.S. Departments of State and Defense and the U.S. Senate and as a management analyst on the staff of President Julius Nyerere of Tanzania under the auspices of the Ford Foundation. He holds an A.B. from Princeton's Woodrow Wilson School of Public and International Affairs, a J.D. from the University of Michigan Law School, and a Ph.D. from the Soviet Center at Pennsylvania State University. He was a Visiting Scholar at the Kennan Institute for Advanced Russian Studies in 1979 and at the Hoover Institution in 1988. He is the author of *The Supreme Soviet: Politics and the Legislative Process in the Soviet Political System* and numerous monographs and articles on Soviet involvement in Africa.